michael curran

michael curran

with essays by trish lyons and jim mooney

film and video umbrella

minigraph 5

First published 2003 by Film and Video Umbrella
52 Bermondsey Street London SE1 3UD
Tel: 020 7407 7755
Fax: 020 7407 7766
HTTP://www.fvumbrella.com

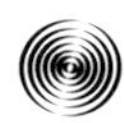

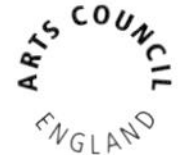

This publication was supported by the National Lottery through the Arts Council of England

ISBN 1 90427 003 4

Edited by Steven Bode
Editorial Assistance by Nina Ernst
Design by Claudia Schenk
Printed and bound in Great Britain

British Library Cataloguing in Publication Data: a CIP record for this publication is available from the British Library

contents

holey swarmings

trish lyons

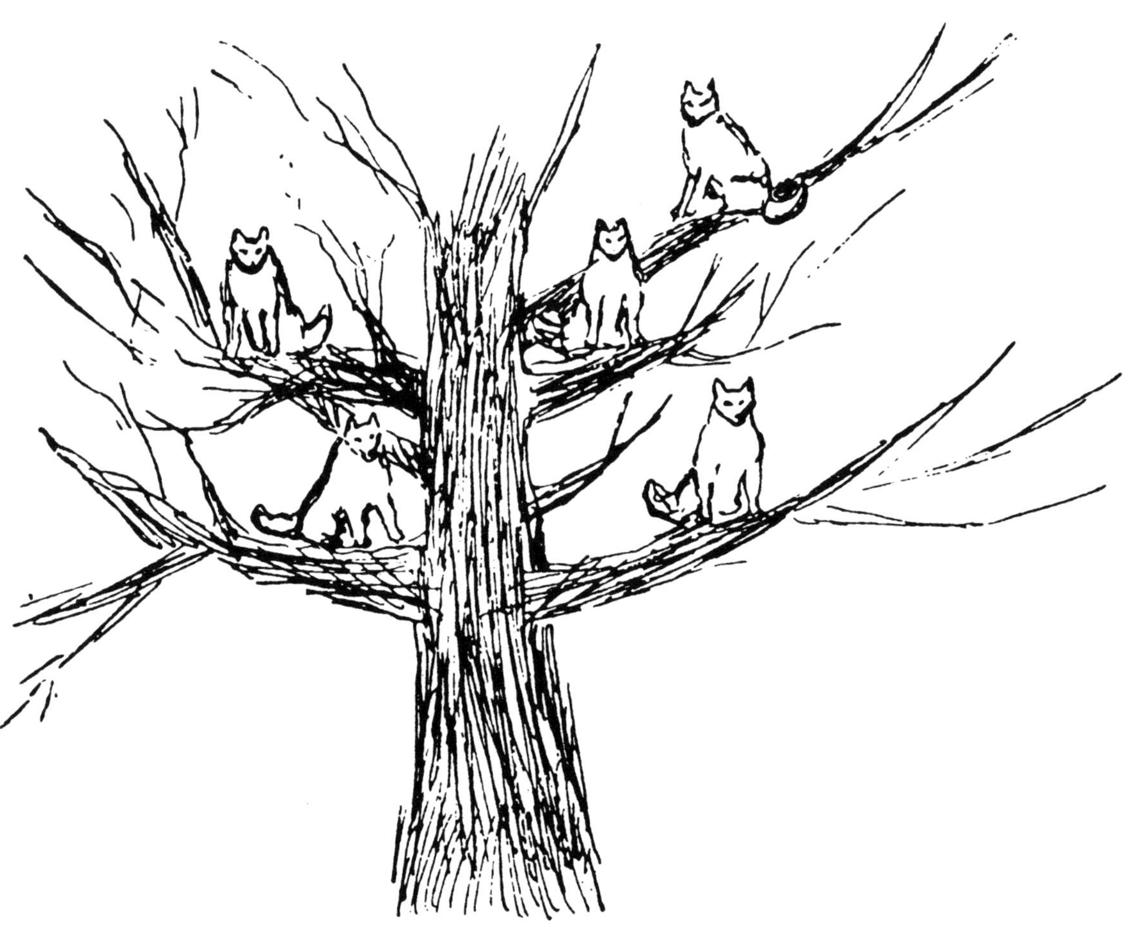

> Method for understanding images, symbols etc. Not to try to interpret them but to look at them till the light suddenly dawns. [1]
> Simone Weil

Imagine, if you will, that the full stop that marks the end of this sentence is not a dot but instead is a cross-section of a horizon line. Following along this line of thinking, and allowing this horizon to be limited to the last ten years, we would then have a ground from which we can draw a set of characters and events. For the time being, allow these characters and events to be those portrayed in the videos of Michael Curran. To begin our inquiry we must all agree to allow ourselves to become each other, in the same way that an actor takes on a role; the key here is the action of play. This is necessary because we (you, me, Michael and an assortment of shadowy figures) are presently ontologically co-dependant. You are free to leave at any time; simply jump down the first black hole you come to. From this point, we are one; as much alike as the left hand is to the right. As close as we seem, though, we will still remain separate and alone. Alone in the way that you are alone in a crowded cinema, engrossed in a film that seems to have been made just for you.

WHO ARE WE?

In the video *Disclaimer* we see a closely-framed shot of a woman's face. She speaks with a foreign accent and appears to be weeping as she recites the disclaimer of the title;

> The characters and events portrayed in this videotape are entirely fictional. Any resemblance to persons known either living or dead is purely coincidental.

There are repeated takes, each time with a slightly different emphasis on the words she is reciting. Sometimes she wipes her eyes. Her tears are clearly visible. In one take we hear Curran say off-camera; 'that's too much'. Is it because she is over-acting, or is he asking to her to moderate an all-too-real excess of emotion? Ambiguity is at the heart of the work. Is she crying because she cannot live up to the director's exacting demands or, more simply, because of the fierce, blinding light shining directly in her eyes? One way or other, there is no proof of her identity, only a growing confirmation of the extent to which a persona is constructed; instilled through interaction, reinforced by repetition.

We encounter the figure of The Foreign Woman again in *Translation*, *Mutter*, *Fistula*, *Natalya* and *Love in a Cold Climate*. A character that inhabits the space of 'the other', she is simultaneously the same as us and different from us. Her identity is not fixed; rather, it is formed through a set of relations. Her capacity to transform is shared by other characters that recur in the videos:

A Transvestite:
Alabama Song, *Larynx*, *Les souffrances du dubbing*

Foucault's Look-alike:
Panopticon, *Natalya*

A Child:
All My Little Ducks, *Natalya*, *Love in a Cold Climate*

A Talking Machine:
Demonstration, *Fistula*

Animals:
Das Pelzchen, *The Small Boy's Dream*, *Alabama Song*, **footnote*, *Love in a Cold Climate*

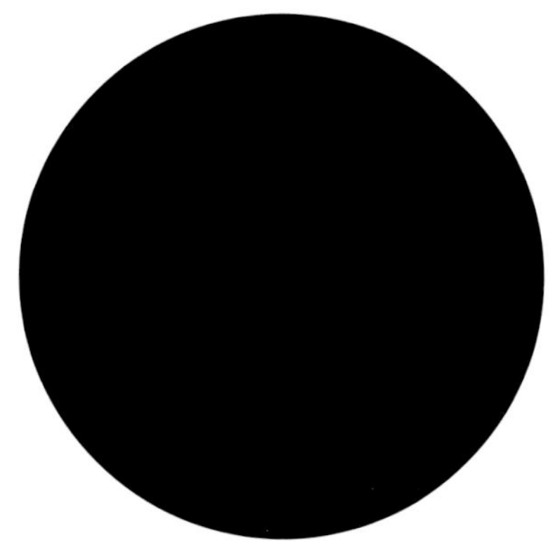

Each of these characters exists on the borders of identity. A man becomes a woman, a look-alike becomes a double, a child becomes an adult, an animal or machine becomes human. Although the means differ, for example maturation or anthropomorphism, they all share the capacity to transform.

In *Les souffrances du dubbing*, a transvestite appears in front of an artificial waterfall, by means of a blue screen. Her exaggerated appearance compounded by her dislocation produces an intense artificiality. She is taking great care in positioning herself to ensure that her face is captured in the best possible light. She then begins to lip synch, but the edits are such that it is difficult to hear what she is saying. There are repeated takes. Perhaps she is saying something about Spain. We cannot be sure. Is she saying 'anything new lately' or is it 'I've never been there'? Eventually, we are able to make out the question: 'Has Spinoza written anything new lately?'

Through a geometry of negation we confront the artifice of identity; she is neither a man nor a woman, she is not speaking with her own voice and she is not saying what we think she is saying.

Les souffrances du dubbing takes its title from an essay by Antonin Artaud. In this essay Artaud considers the effect of dubbing as a form of grotesque ventriloquism. For Artaud, real actors embody thought and feeling. They act out their voice, physique, charm and sex appeal. Thus the torments of dubbing come from the sacrifice of the personality of the real actor for the sake of an artificial personality. The artifice in *Les souffrances du dubbing* can therefore be seen as a witty corrective to the false projection of identity to which the representational subject is prone.

Apart from Sissy in *Fistula* and Natalya in *Natalya* and *Love in a Cold Climate*, no one has a proper name. Instead, characters operate as ciphers performing an action: someone looking at a painting, someone digging a hole, someone mixing records, someone reciting a text, someone singing, someone skipping, someone shadow boxing, someone talking, someone laughing, someone shattering a mirror. They are singled out by the camera and appear alone. They are actors as agents of actions rather than actors as agents of dialogue.

Repetition is embedded in each of these actions. We see this in the dancers learning a dance in *Panopticon* and *Rush*; and the actors repeating their lines in *Panopticon*, *Disclaimer* and *Natalya*. Repetition is not just a means of learning a role but can also be a process of mastering and overcoming ourselves. In *Untitled/Skipping*, we see a naked man with a shaved head, alone in a room. He is skipping on the spot while repeating the words: 'when you fall like a stone, one must not think; if one thinks, then one must not fall.' Initially, he starts and stops. Then he manages to get a sustained rhythm going. We hear the whipping sound of the rope as it slices the air. The overall effect is hypnotic. It services the action of transcending gravity, moving beyond the senses and finally escaping the self.

HOW DO WE BECOME EACH OTHER?

> I dreamt that it was night and that I was lying in my bed. Suddenly the window opened of its own accord, and I was terrified to see some white wolves... There were six or seven of them. The wolves were quite white... their ears pricked liked dogs when they pay attention to something. In great terror, evidently of being eaten up by the wolves, I screamed... It seemed as though they had riveted their whole attention on me.[2]
>
> Freud's notes recording a session with The Wolf-Man

Looking at The Wolf-Man's drawing of his dream, one cannot help but be struck by the five pairs of eyes staring out from the picture. The longer one looks at the drawing the more intense the staring becomes. The ten little dots bore holes into the viewer and become black holes in the picture. It is one thing to be looked at, quite another to be subject to such a penetrating stare.

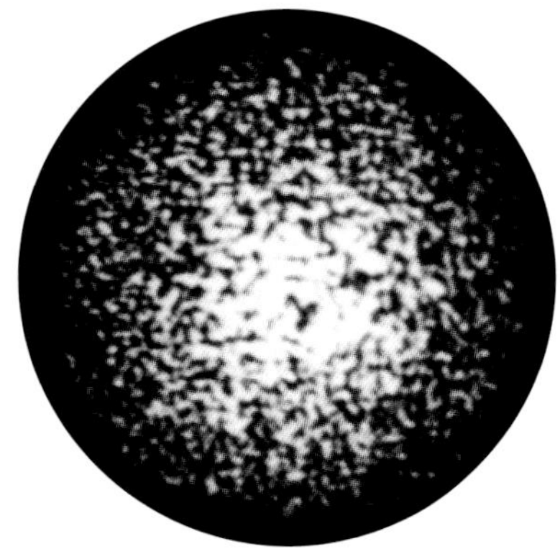

There are other holes, of course, that can provide a point of entry: lover's holes, through which we become wholly porous to one another; sound holes through which we are penetrated by, and absorbed into, music. We hear of white holes in *Love in a Cold Climate*, as we watch bright white snowflakes swirl in the night air. In the fairy tale, 'The Snow Queen', a boy and a girl are next-door neighbours. Hans Christian Andersen tells us that they were such good friends that they were like brother and sister. He further emphasises the intensity of their friendship by telling us that their rooftop windows faced each other. In the winter the windows were thick with frost, but the two children would warm up a coin on the stove, then press it on the frozen pane making a peephole. Behind each round hole was an eye, one at each window. These holes transform into an image of swarming white bees as the grandmother tells the children about the Snow Queen. We hear this fragment of the story in *Love in a Cold Climate* over the white noise of a television screen which appears as a vibrating field of white, light spots.

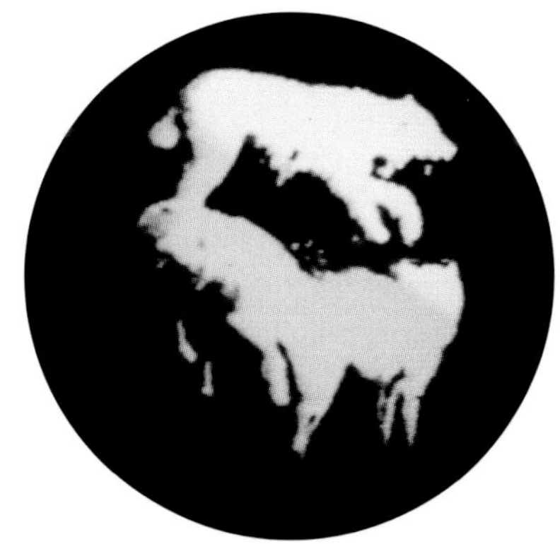

Alabama Song begins with a hole in the screen through which we see a transvestite. She flirts and teases the viewer. The hole then becomes a full moon which dissolves to reveal a pack of wolves. We hear growling and snarling while through the hole we look down upon a pair of bare feet walking swiftly over a dark ground. As these images transform there is a text which reads:

> You're here
> obey or bite
> bite or obey
> caught in the act

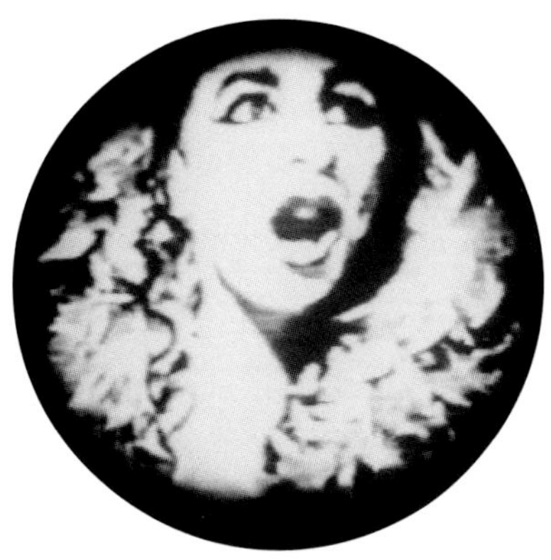

We are reminded of the action of being caught.

Alabama Song illustrates how Curran plays with light in order to perform the tricks of transformation. The high contrast black-and-white images are either over-exposed, which wipes out detail, or under-exposed, which creates deep shadow. He sometimes uses a single light source to create high-relief images. These effects produce a play between light and shadow much in the same way that disruptive patterning works in camouflage. Images appear and disappear, animated and transformed by movement; shape-shifting before our eyes.

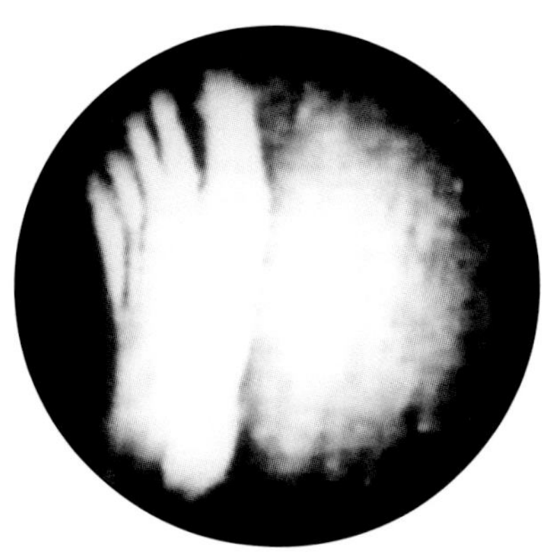

Imagine, if you will, that the full stop that marks the end of this sentence is not a dot but a hole, which we, all of us, pass through...We are a holey swarming of dappled light. We become each other as a bird in a flock, a wolf in a pack. We are a multitude disguised as a singularity.

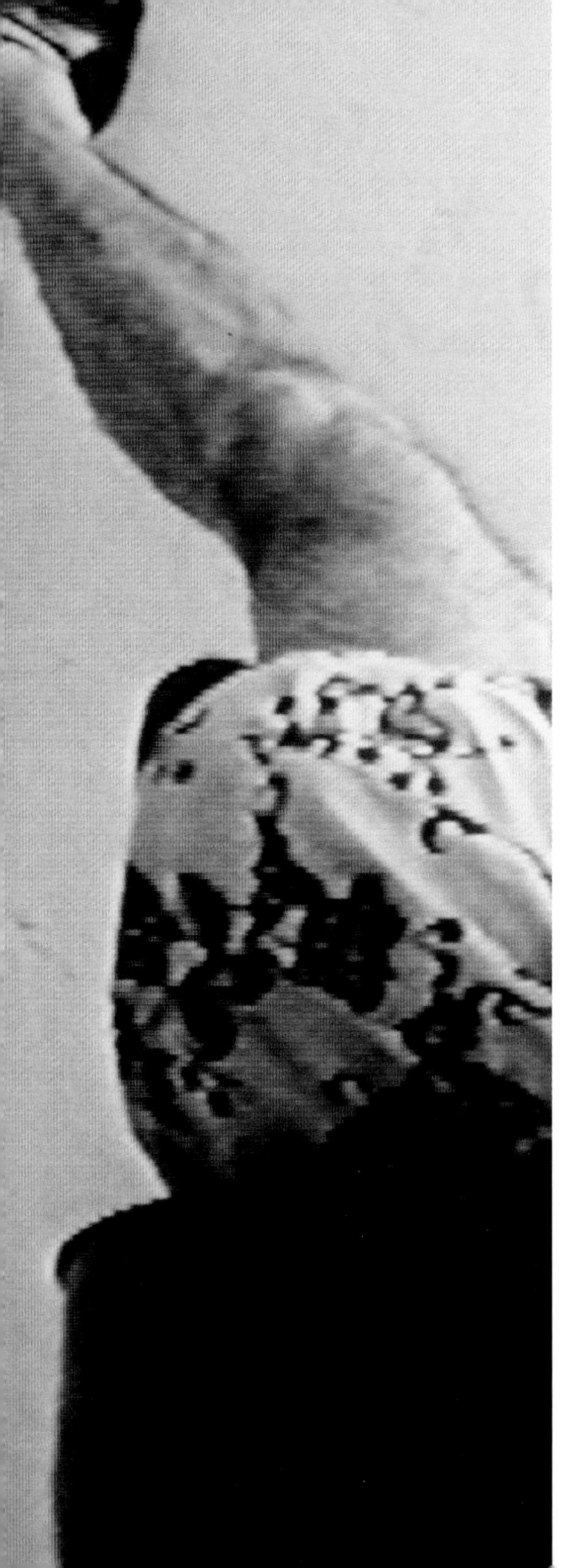

> May I disappear in order that those things that I see may become perfect in their beauty from the very fact that they are no longer things that I see. [3]
> Simone Weil

In *Portfolio* we are confronted with an image of Curran's face seen upside down and framed by the v-shape spread of his legs. Apart from his shoes and his shirt he is naked. His hair is shorn, emphasising the shape of his head. The video is one continuous take, which lasts as long as it takes him to masturbate. As he approaches climax his face becomes increasingly red and his expression is strained. He blinks and squints. The voice-over lists a series of drawings, giving the title and the medium. The drawings are taken from an exhibition curated by Jacques Derrida entitled 'Memoirs of the Blind':

> Study of the Blind
> Christ Healing a Blind Man
> The Error
> Truth Unveiled by Time
> The Senses
> Self Portrait
> Narcissus
> With Closed Eyes
> Head of a Dying Man
> Head of Medusa
> Cyclops
> Severed Head
> Weeping
> Head Study etc.

The composition is such that it does not focus on the act of masturbation (the repeated practice of which, it's said, will make us go blind), but rather the large, inverted, red and straining head emerging out of a pair of legs, which suggests we are watching a birth; a birth that doubles as a little death.

Fistula, a collaboration with Osnat Haber, tells the story of an ill-fated love affair, but also tells of the fate of the writer who is eternally bound into a struggle of mastery over, and/or enslavement to, the word. The narration of the story is provided by a tool for the blind, a speaking word-processor; a machine that repeats back to the writer what is written. Its machinic voice has a coldness that enforces the necessary cruelty essential to enslavement. We are told of a love affair that was doomed from the beginning. There is no sense of tragedy; rather a masochistic desire for the beautiful Sissy, something that Sissy will never understand. In her refusal to be mastered, the lover becomes entangled in her own desire. The video itself is looped so there is no beginning or ending, compounding a sense of eternal recurrence. *Fistula* presents to us a series of images of different women, young and old, caught in various actions. We hear snippets of conversations. We see pieces of yarn, strips of film, strands of hair; fragments of lives caught, reeled and cut onto videotape.

It is the storyteller who grasps these threads of different lives, fragments of events, and weaves them together. The storyteller, like the writer, is also bound into the weave. This convergence of threads, eternity and fate brings to mind another story. The story of the Cruel Fates: Clotho, Lachesis and Atropos. In the secret darkness of their cave, these three blind hags spun, measured and cut the thread of human life. We see in the clay figure 'Clotho' by Camille Claudel a body that is bound into, and drawn out of, the material ground from which she is made. The thick, bundled strands of wool that entwine her legs and drape across her body congeal into a mass on her head. Her right hand is caught in the wool as she attempts to shift the unmanageable density of material that literally pulls the wool over her eyes and blinds her. This is a figure caught and blinded in the very act of its own making. We glimpse a figure such as Clotho in a scene from *Natalya*. On a snow-covered hillside, someone stands with a blanket over their head. The blanket flows to and fro in a slow swinging motion over the swaying figure. The swinging and swaying motions

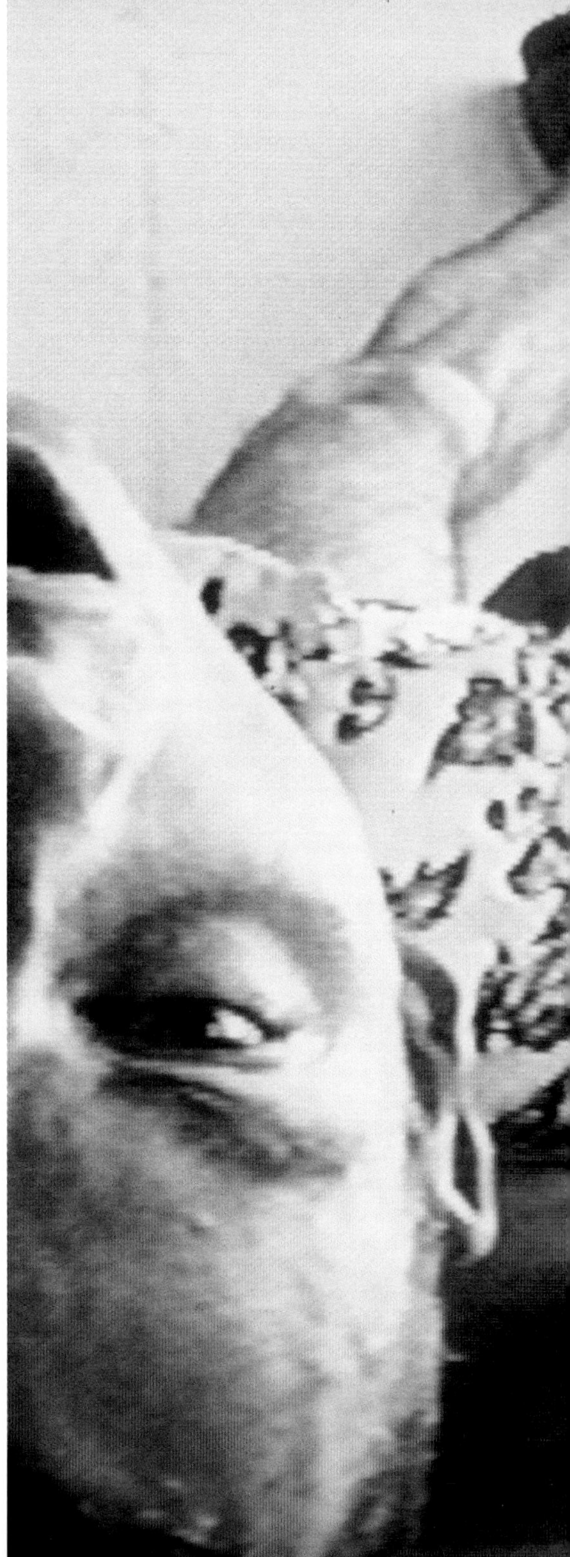

combine to create a contretemps of visual rhythms, while the figure covered in a blanket and the ground covered in snow create a double visual metaphor that folds back on itself; simultaneously concealing and revealing the figure and the ground.

In *Love in a Cold Climate*, a blind storyteller reads the story of the Snow Queen aloud from a text in braille. The white page of braille, to which our gaze is drawn, appears as a snow-covered field. Here we encounter a different blindness; like that of snow blindness, a blinding by light. Light infuses everything in *Love in a Cold Climate*. The light of the full moon provides the opening and closing shots in the video. But there are also flashlights; and light bulbs which switch on and off. Images are lit by the striking of a match or, as if in a slide show, are interspersed with moments of darkness, as the slide projector shutters to the next image. Scenes often end with brilliant whiteness, suggesting a blinking effect. The edits in the videos are timed to echo the blinking of the eyes. This is done consistently, as if to suggest eyesight that is adjusting to blinding light. We can imagine Plato's philosopher squinting upon emerging out of the darkness of the cave. Or Nietzsche's 'last man', who reaches beyond all of his struggles, no longer even able to despise himself, arriving at the end of his journey; 'and he blinks'. We too emerge blinking from the cinema or darkened gallery space. After all that is said and done, it remains that these characters and events are entirely fictional. But the light that finally dawns, which illuminates all of Michael Curran's videos, is fiction's capacity to reveal ourselves.

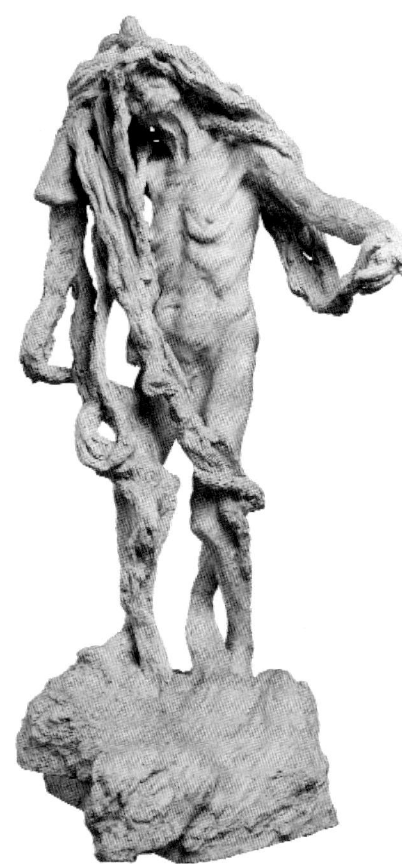

NOTES

1 Simone Weil, 'Self-effacement', *Gravity and Grace*, Routledge, London 2001, page 109

2 Sigmund Freud, 'From the History of an Infantile Neurosis (The "Wolf Man")', *Case Histories II*, Pelican Books 1979, page 259

3 Simone Weil, 'Attention and Will', *Gravity and Grace*, Routledge, London 2001, page 37

PICTURE CREDIT *Clotho* by Camille Claudel, courtesy Musée Rodin, Paris, photograph by Adam Rzepka/ADAGP

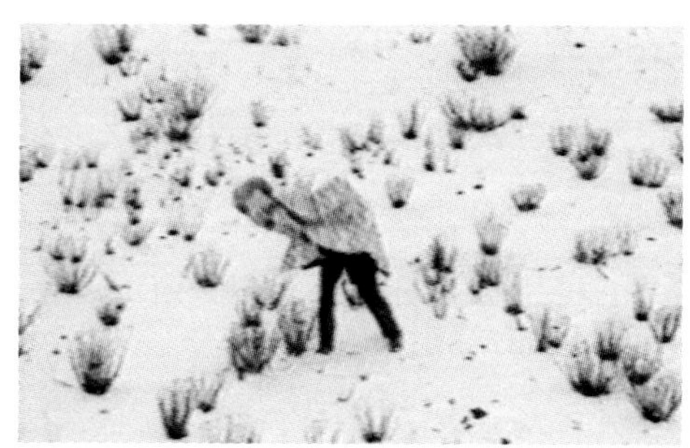

disclaimer

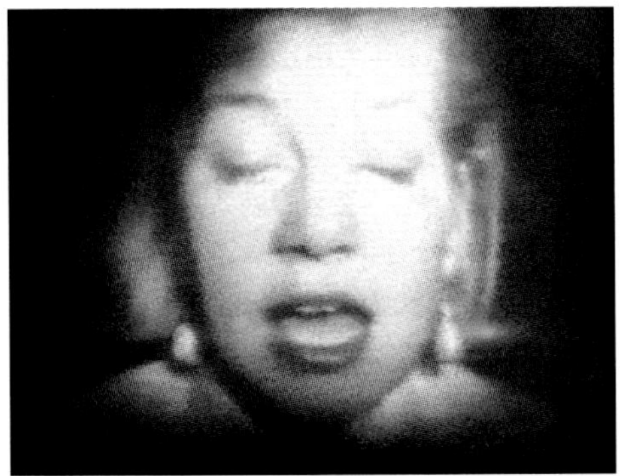

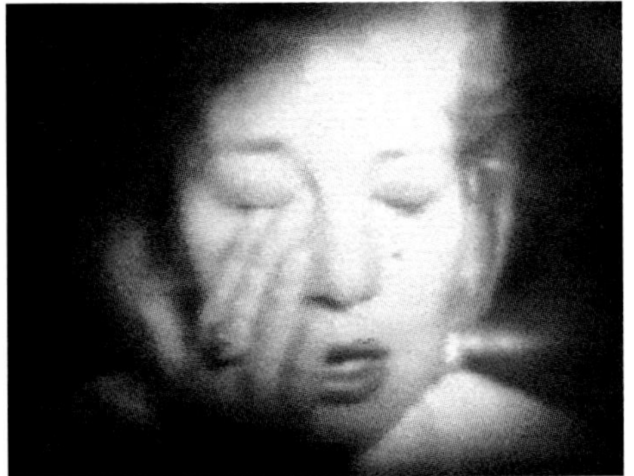

"The characters and events portrayed in this videotape are entirely fictional.
Any resemblance to persons known either living or dead is purely coincidental."

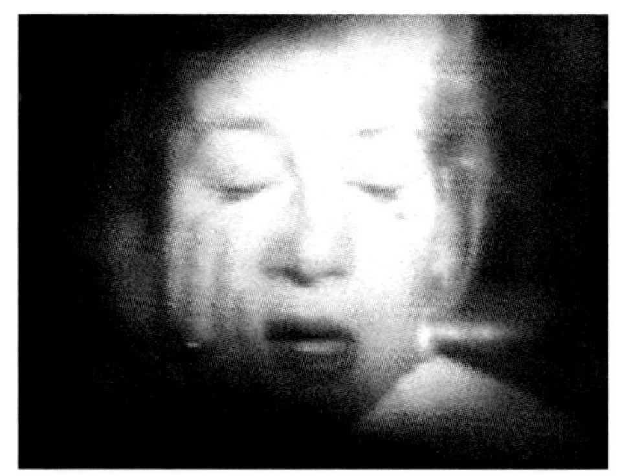
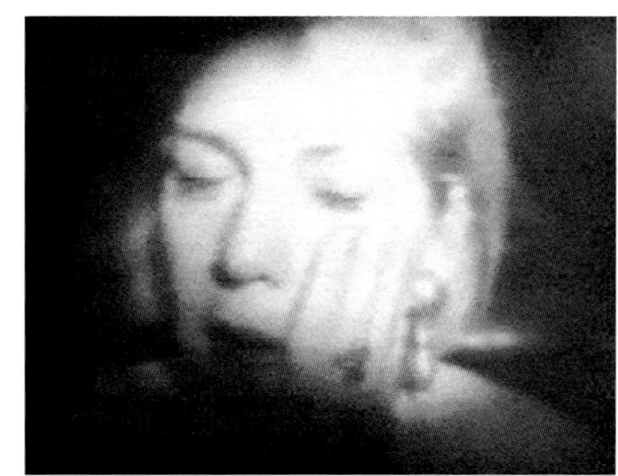
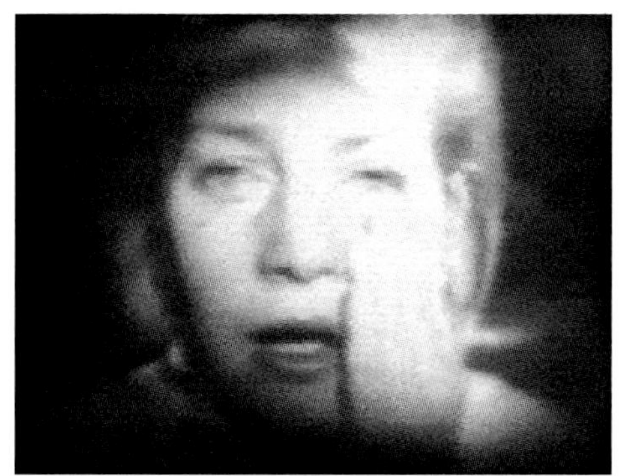
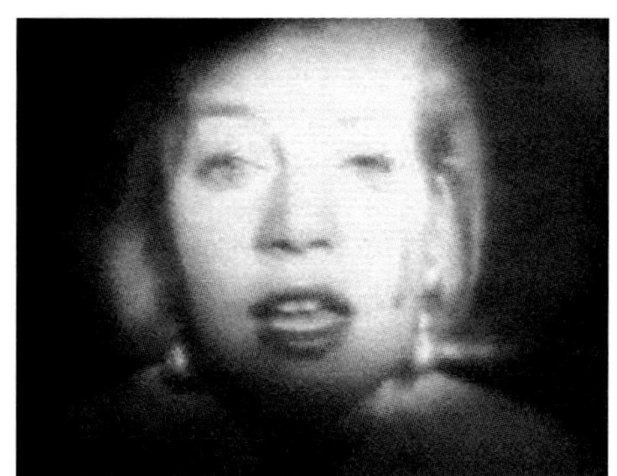

amami se vuoi

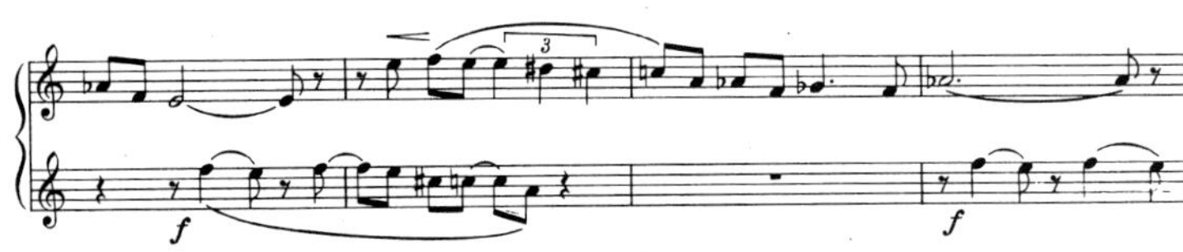

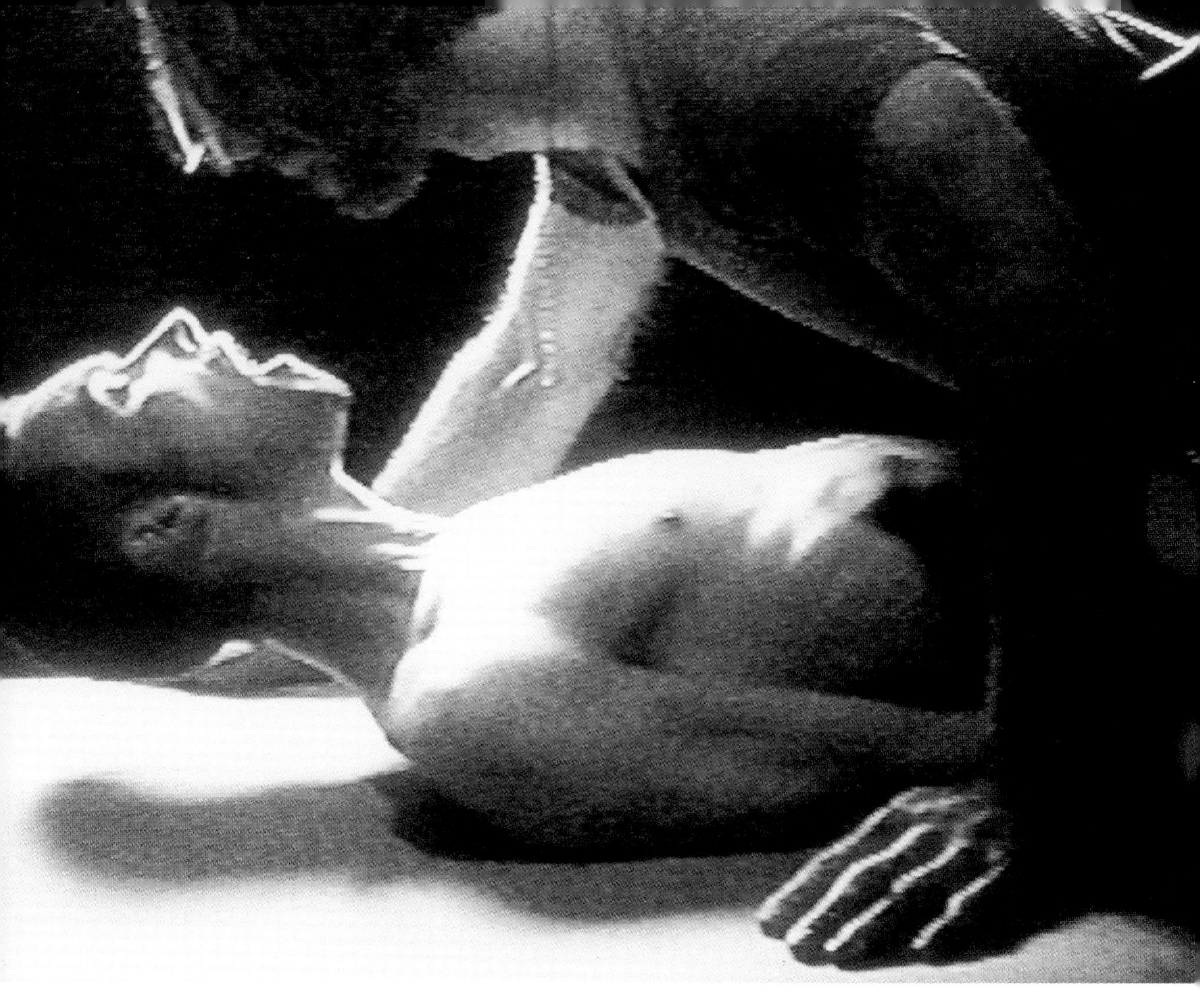

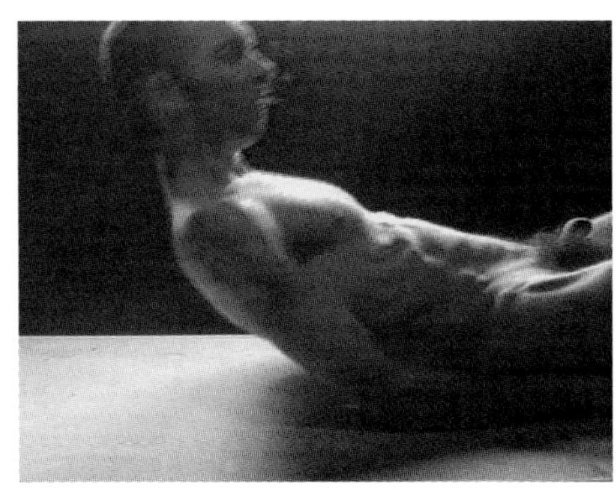

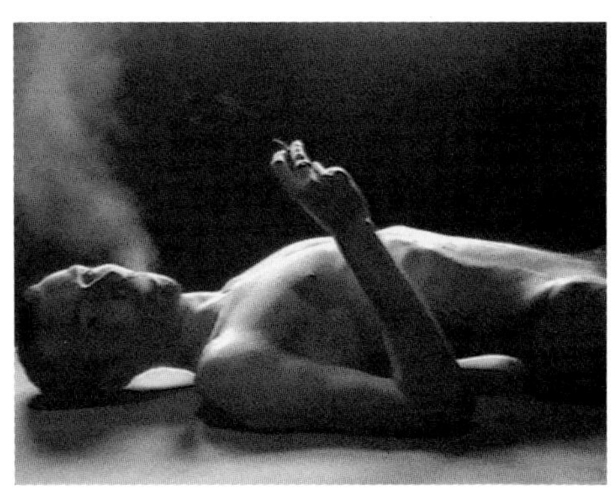

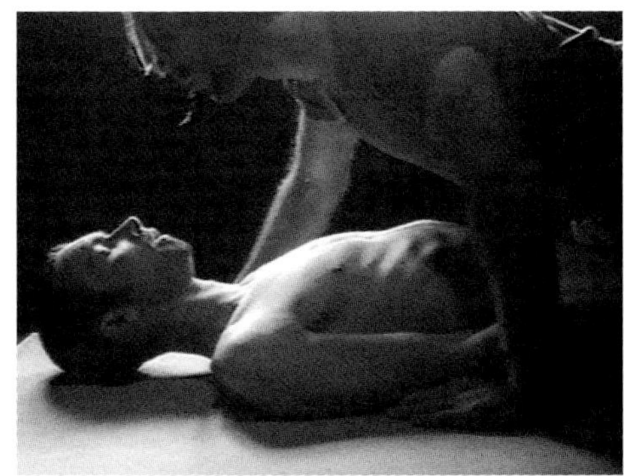

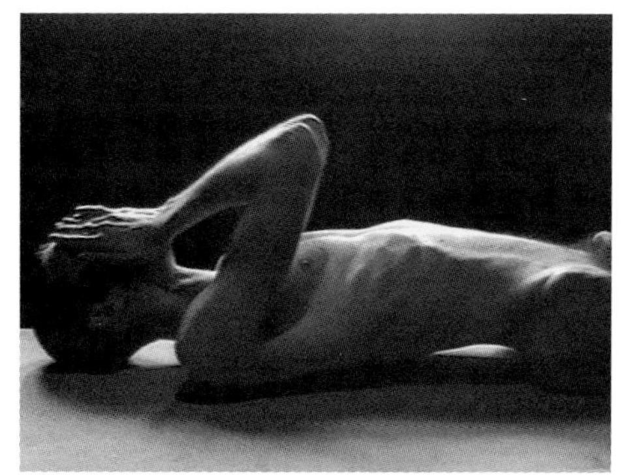

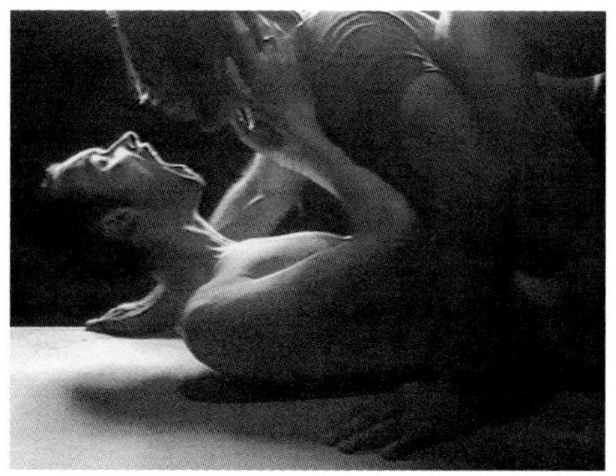

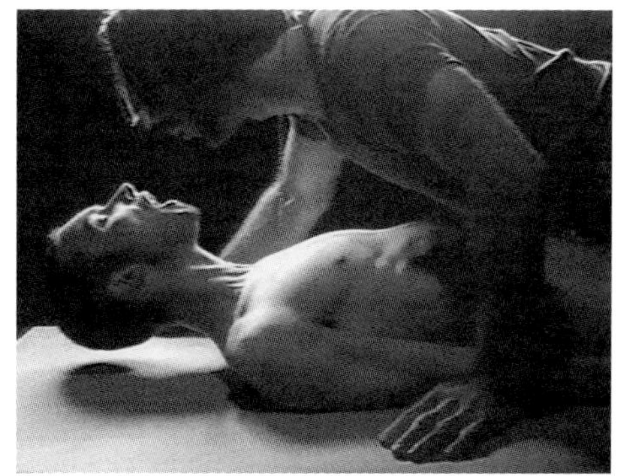

l'heure autosexuelle

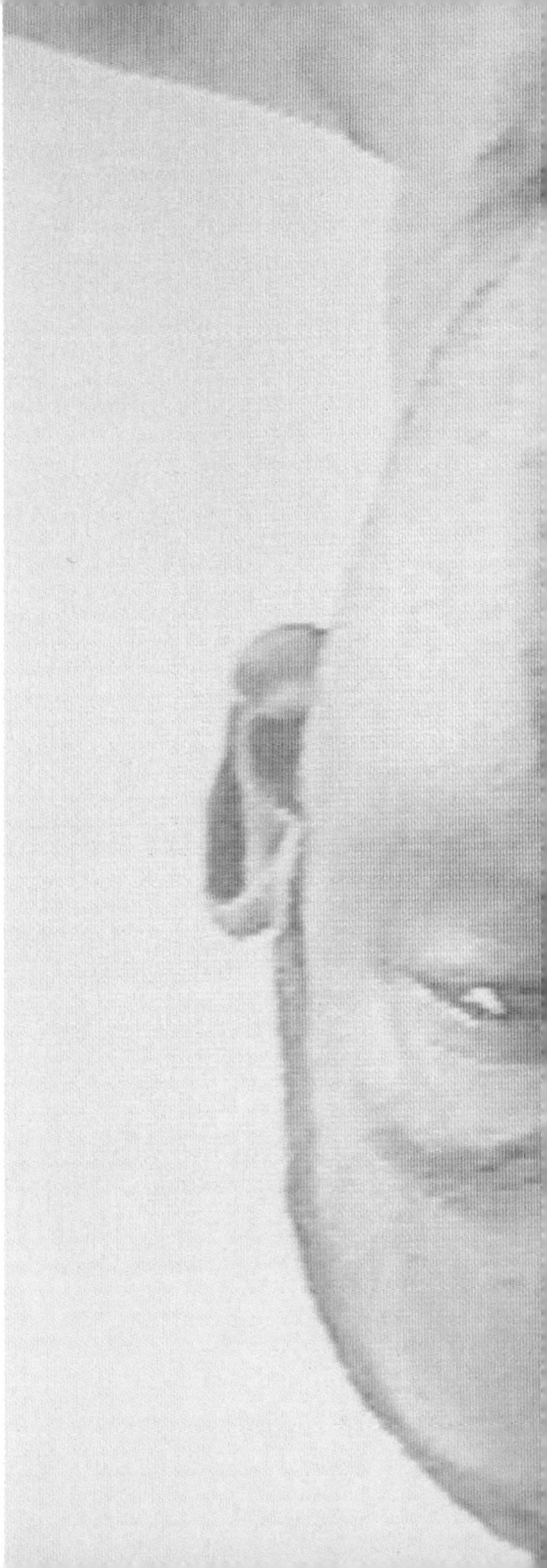

FEAR	Why does your clock have three hands?

LOVE	The first marks the hour, the second urges on the minutes, and the third, forever motionless, eternalises my indifference.

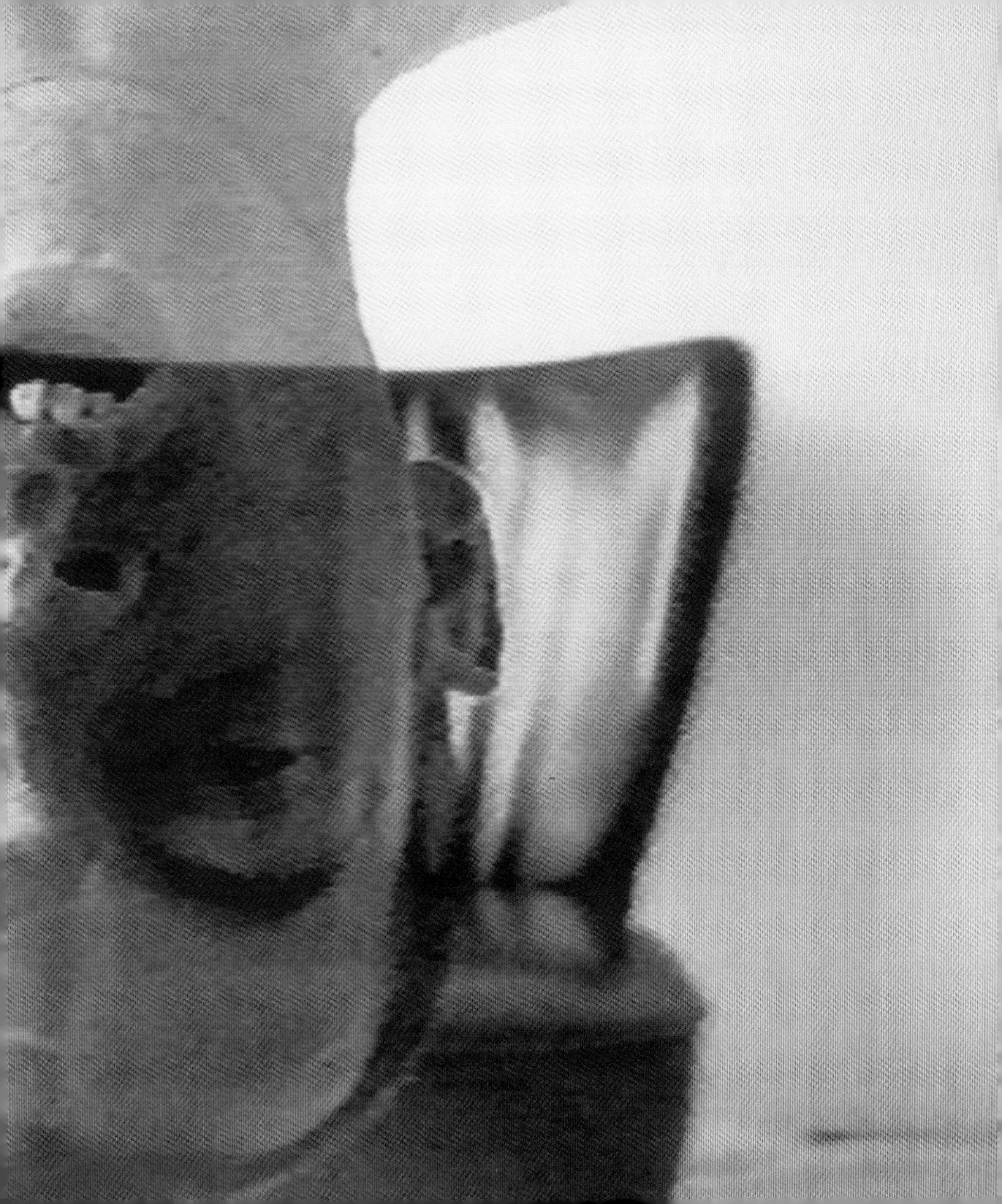

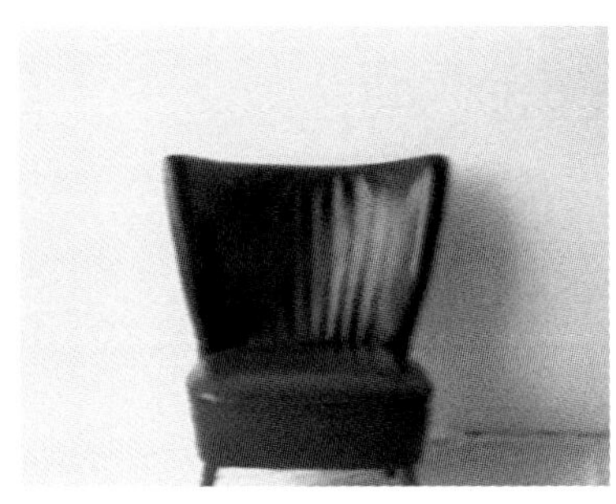

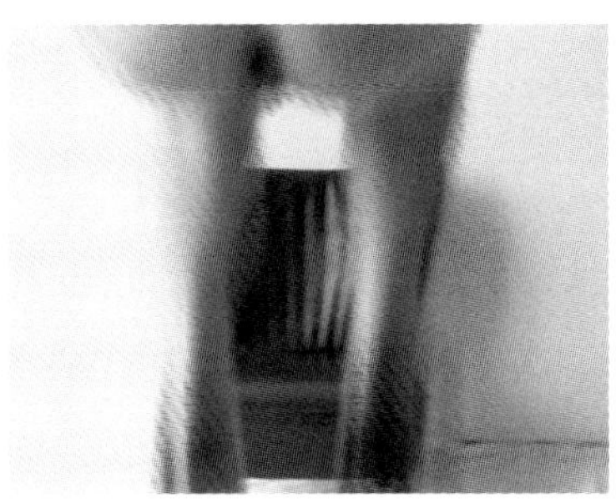

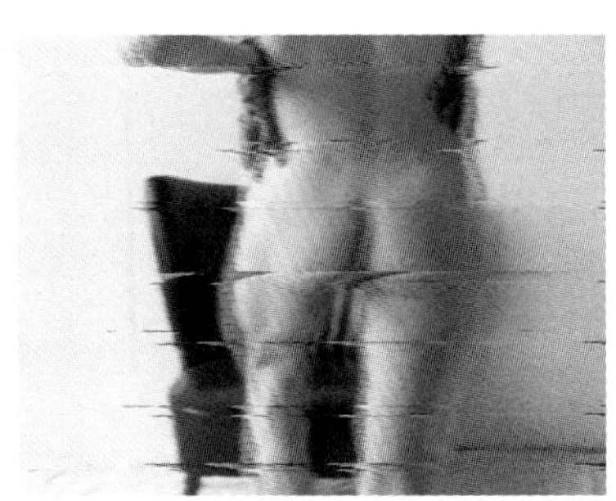

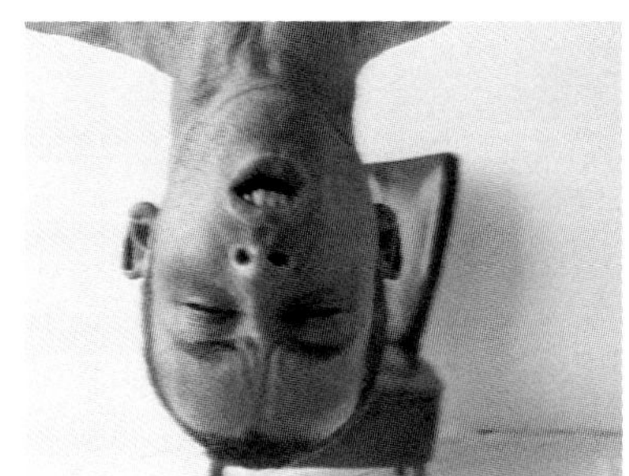

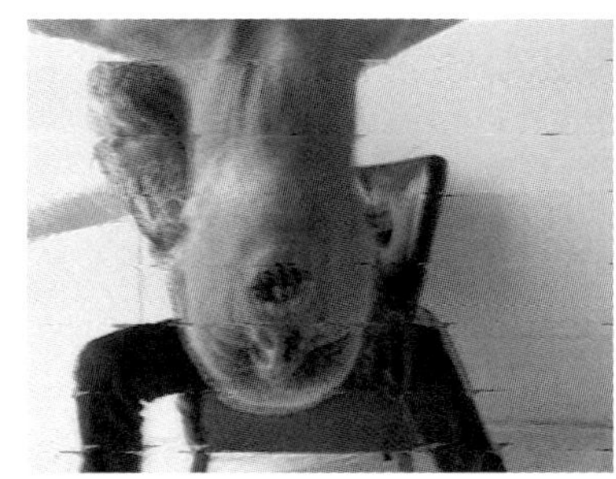

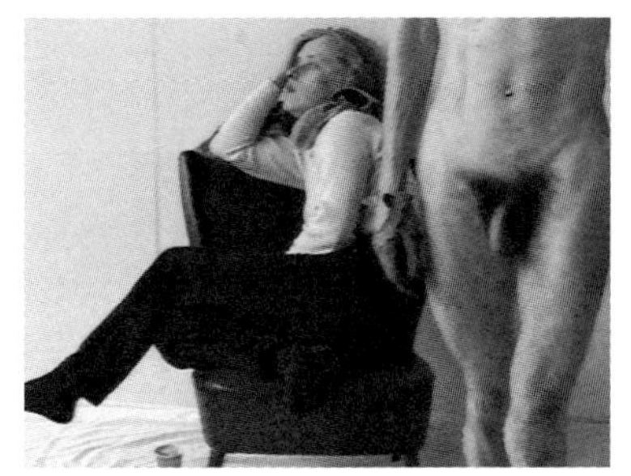

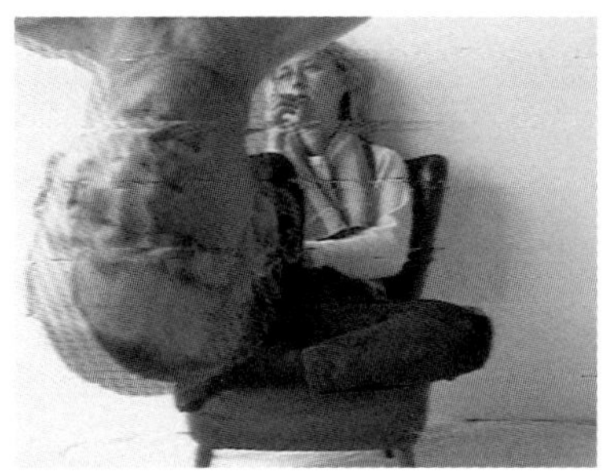

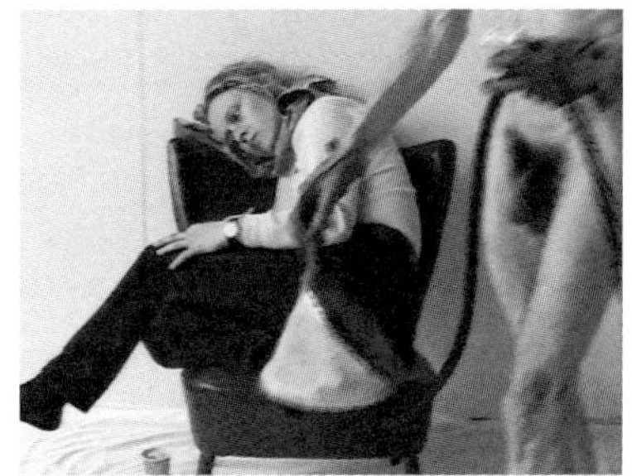

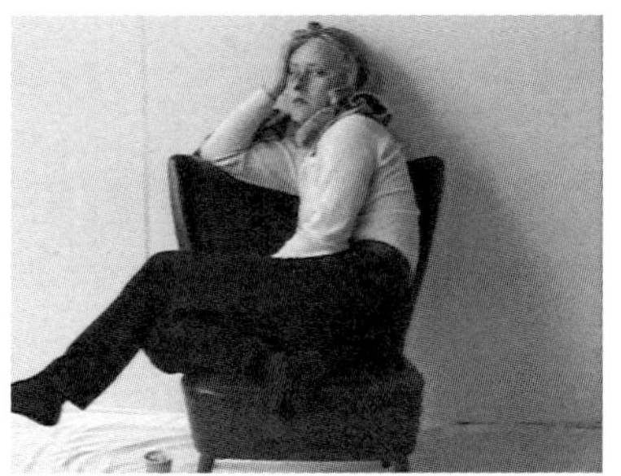

all my little ducks

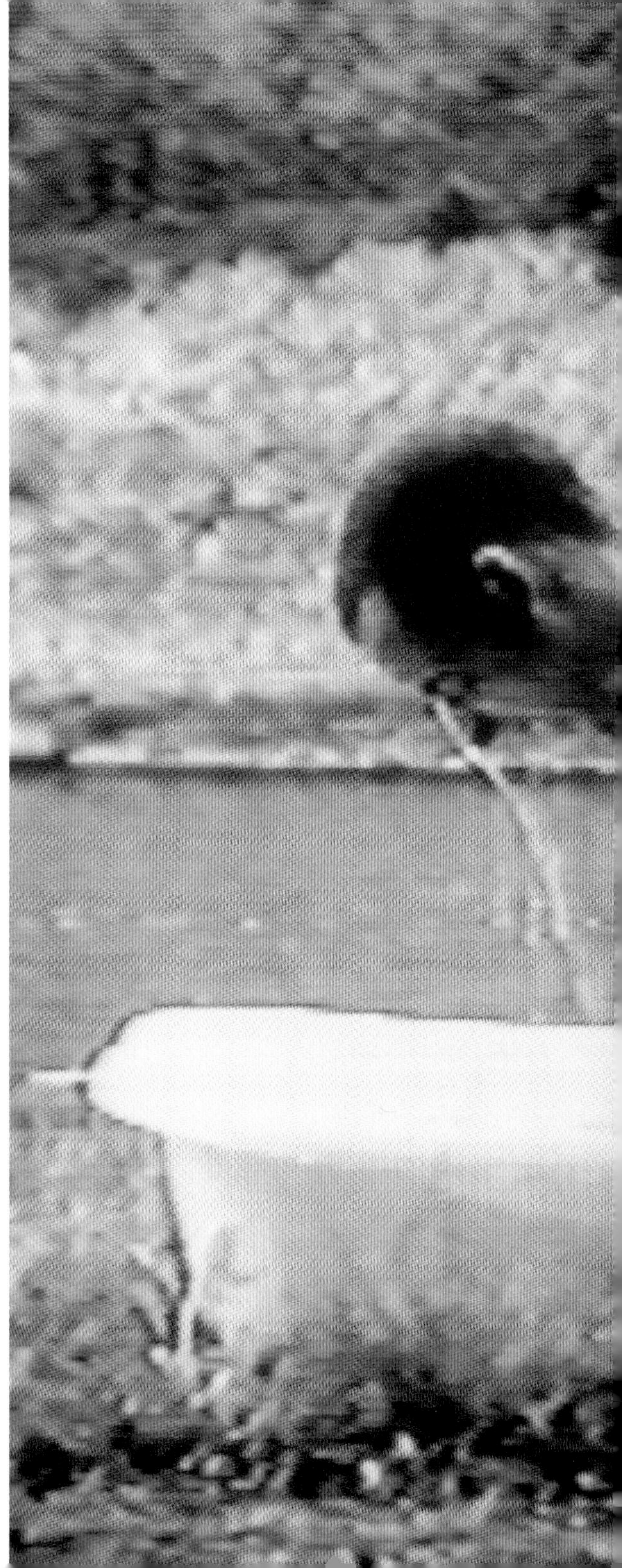

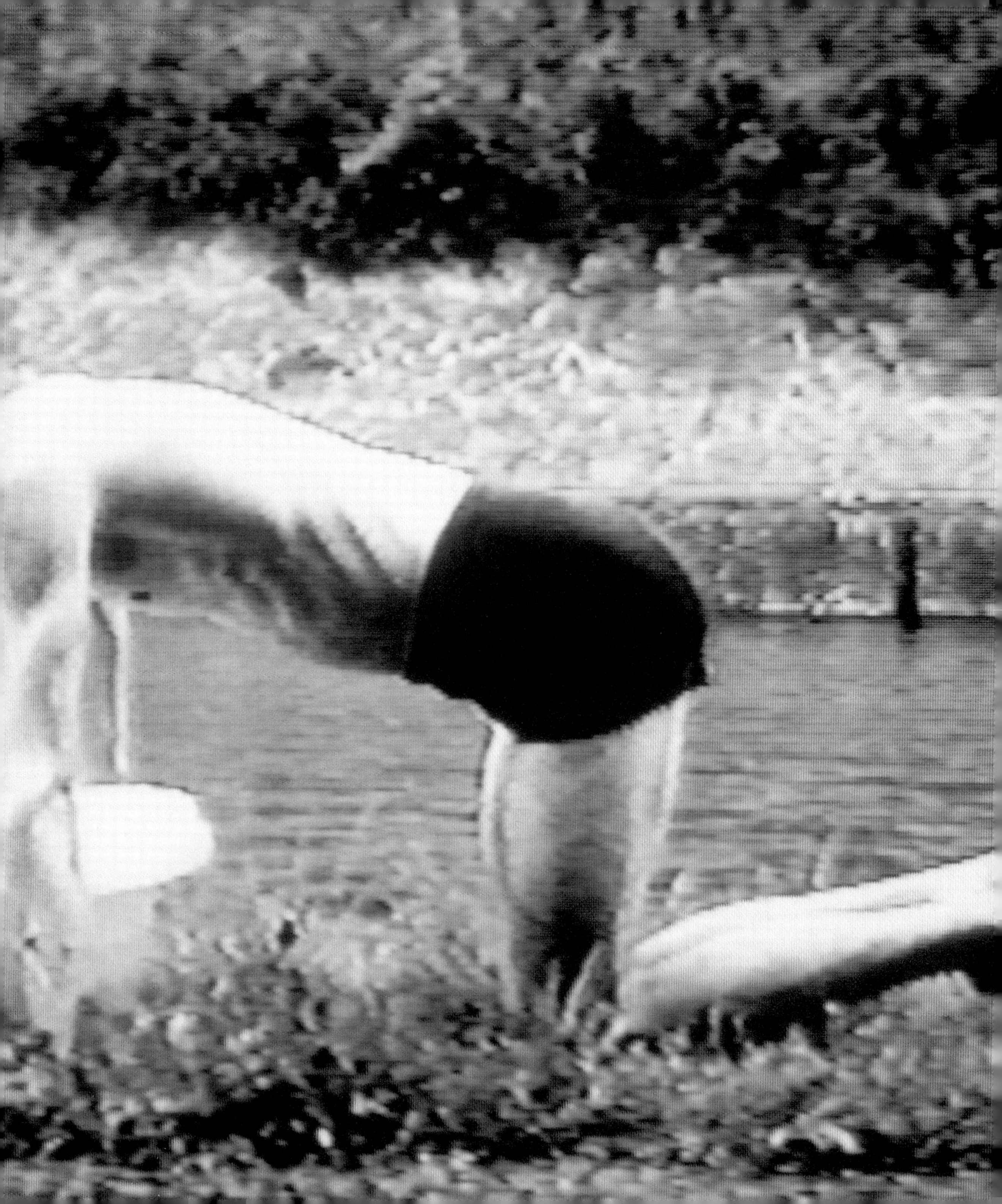

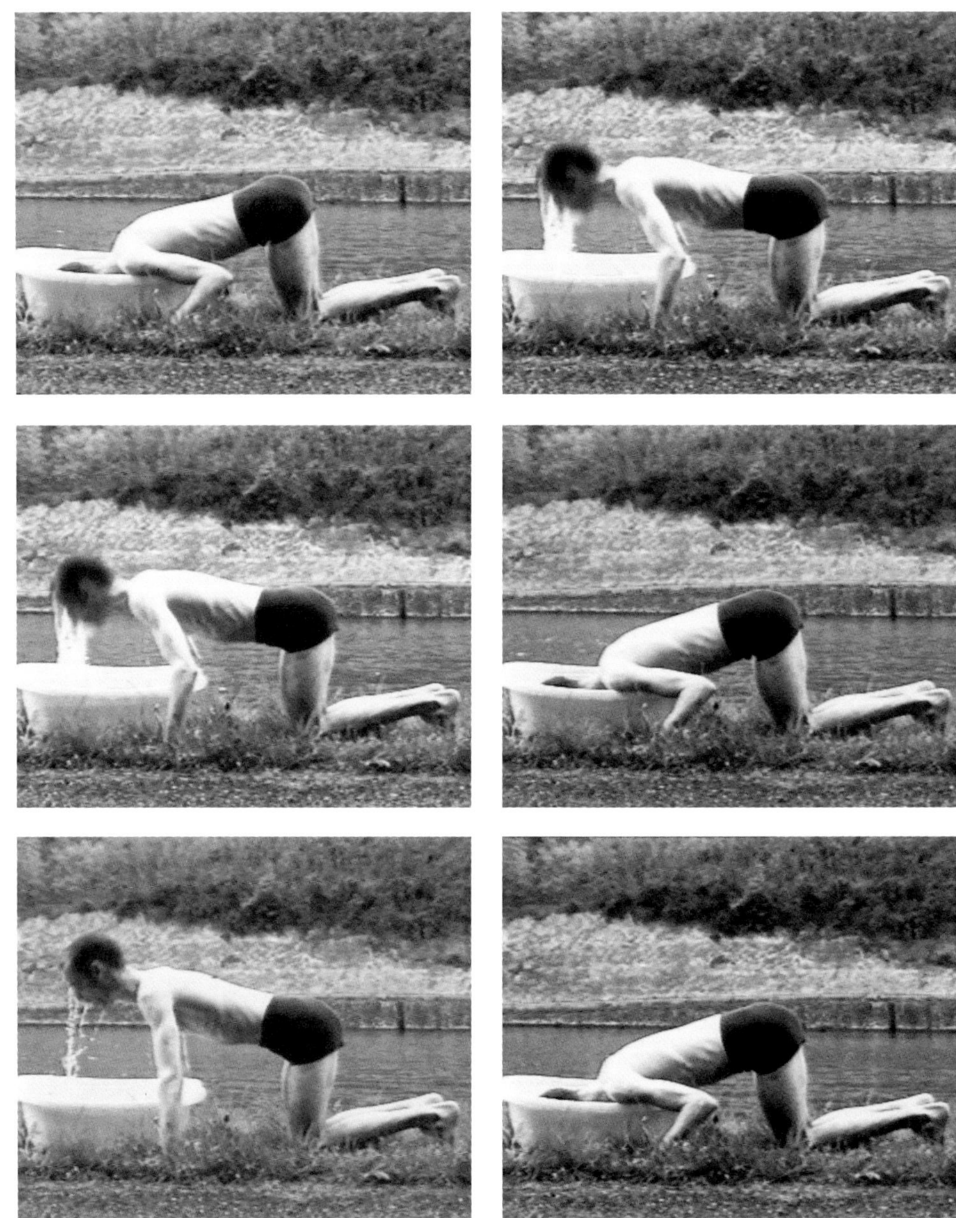

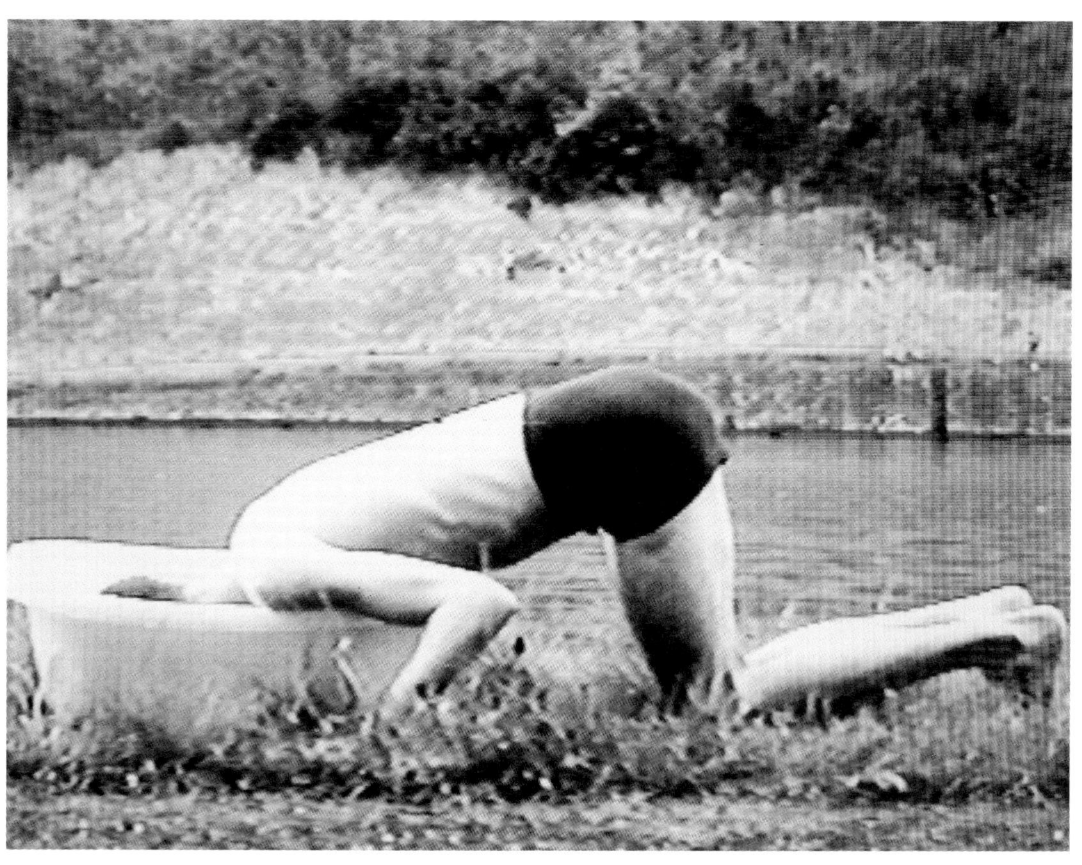

untitled / skipping

When you fall like a stone, one must not think.
If one thinks, then one must not fall.

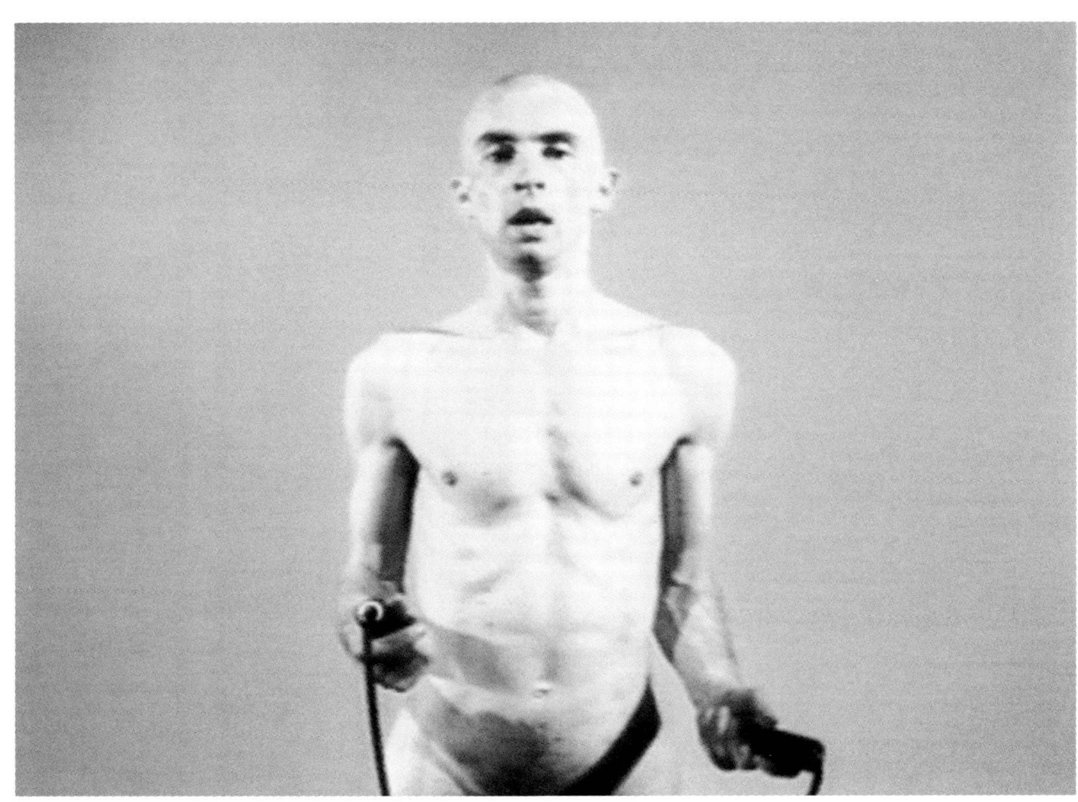

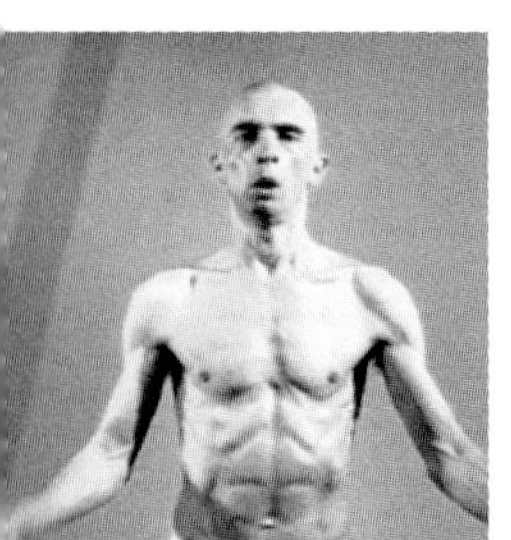
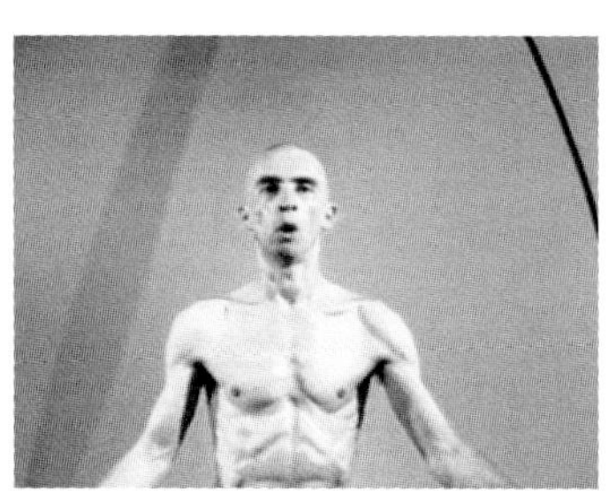
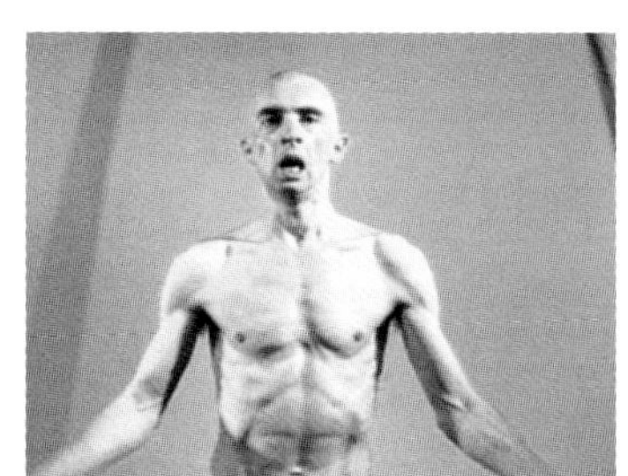
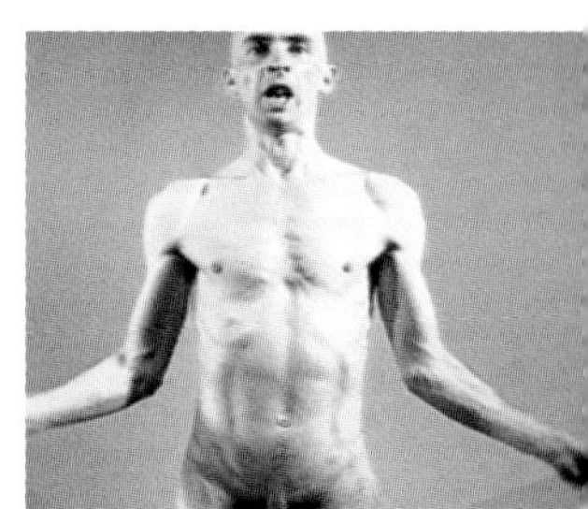

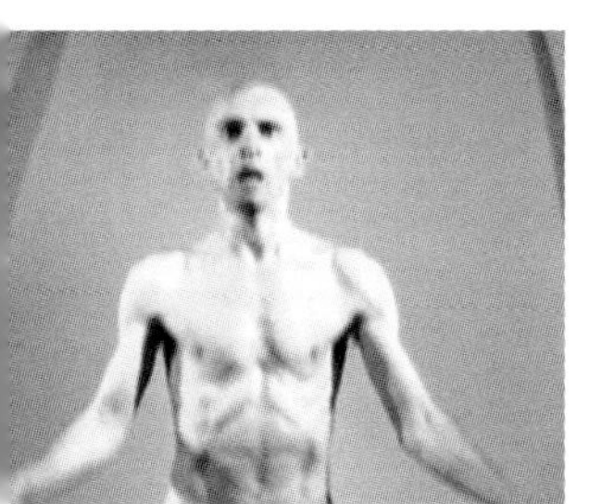
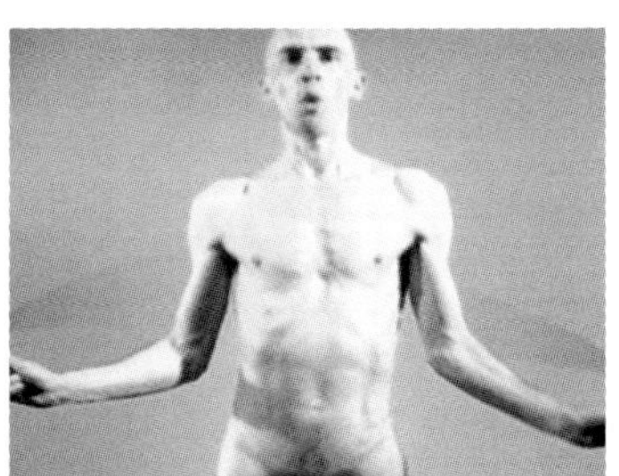
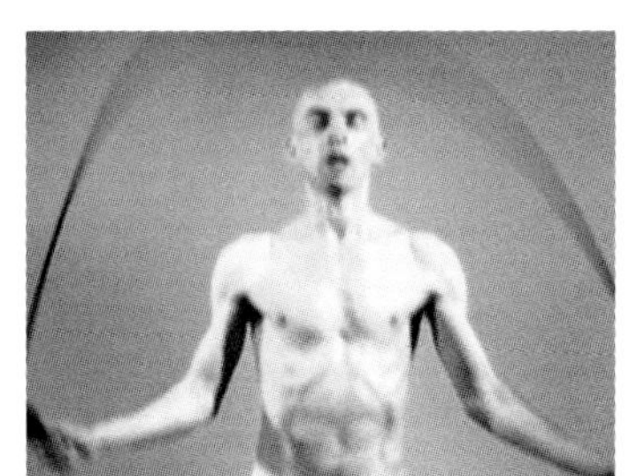
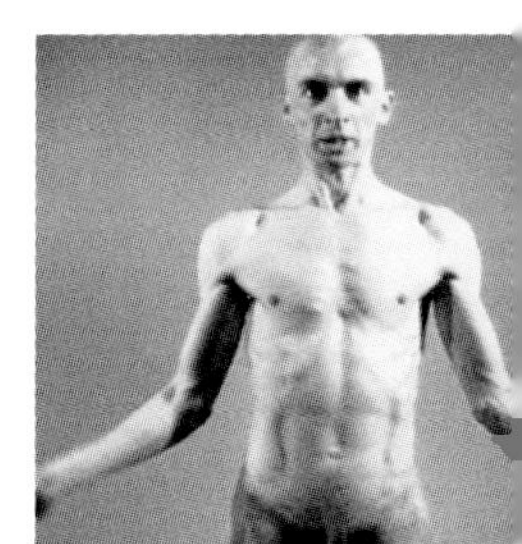

les souffrances du dubbing

How was Spain?

Has Spinoza written anything new lately?

I've never been there, only in my thoughts.

Yes, one can feel nostalgia for a place one has never been.

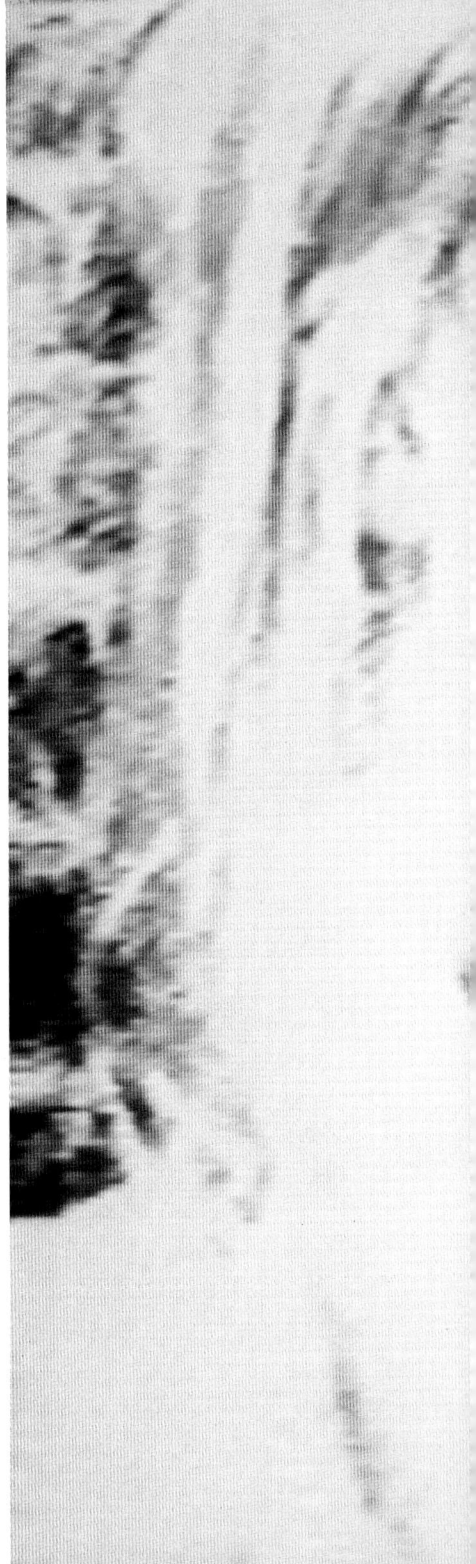

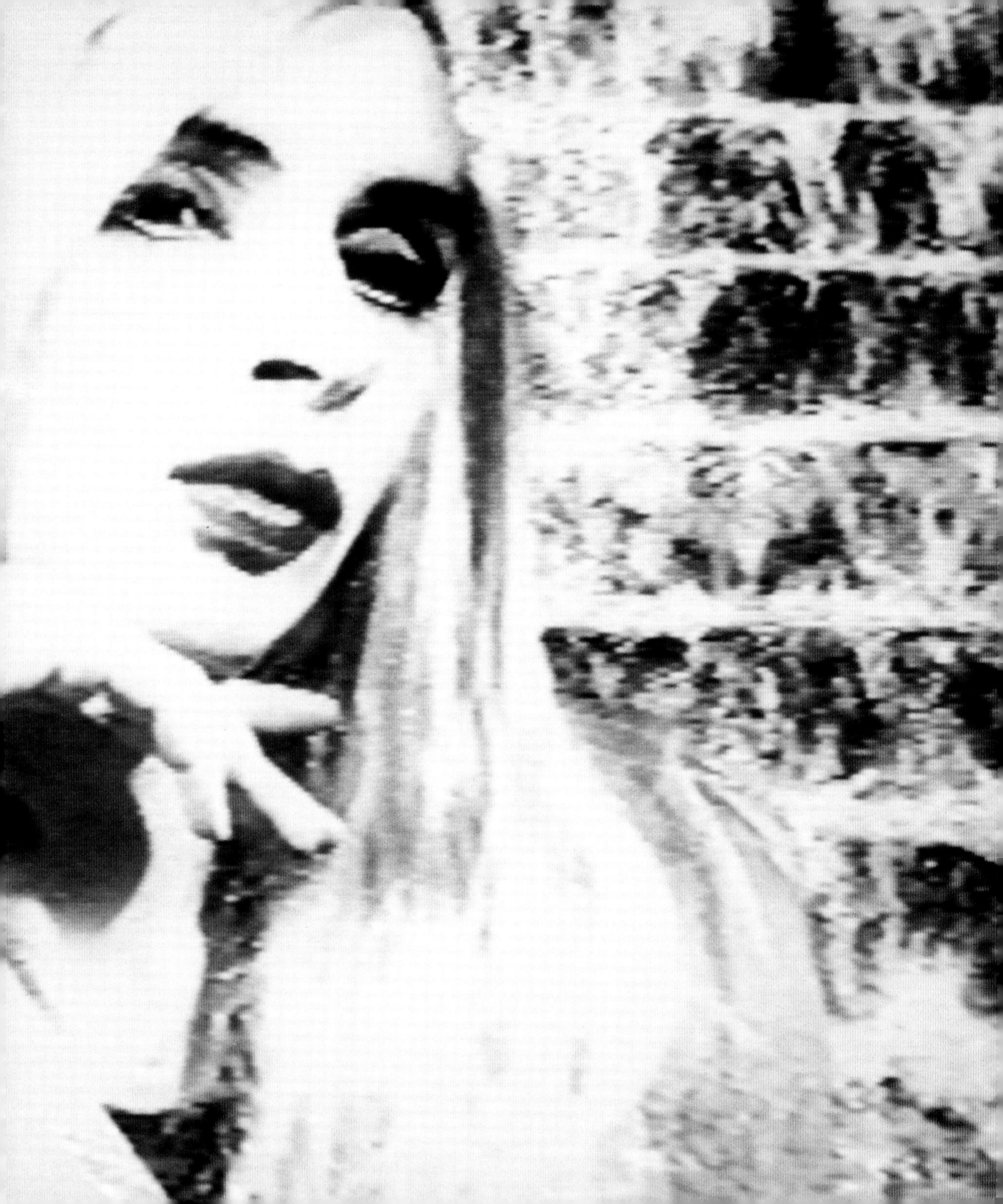

fistula

text osnat haber

The whole idea was to fist her brain.
I've always been good doing that. It was particularly easy with her.
She had the worst haircut I've ever seen: short at the front and far too long along her back, black September short flowery dress.
So many people have died.
An ultimate month to kill people, September is, after all this heat, need to move on, not to be licked off.
Wish it were that simple. She was brought to me Sissy, flowery being, far too much of everything. So I fucked her. Indifferently intercoursed the fucking Sissy's brain and left.

When it hauled up I left.

September is a good month for leaving, I thought, always leave in September, after the heat has come to its peak and all these ice-cream scenarios.
Walking on the street, Sissy is waiting, taking a long coffee, breaking. Sissy is waiting, all the shop windows, telephone booths, prices, flats to rent, no Sissy.

Great life it is indeed.

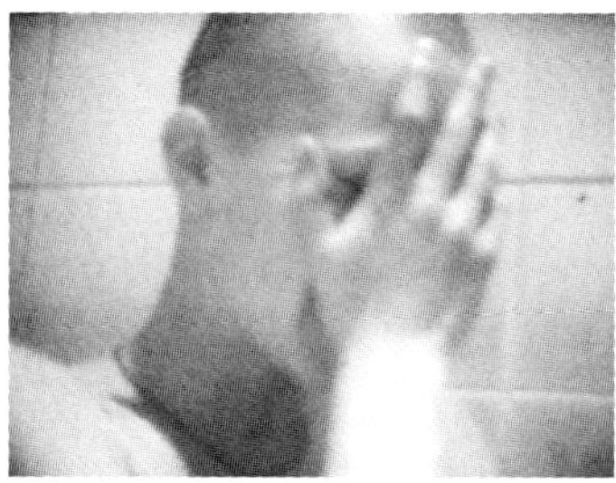

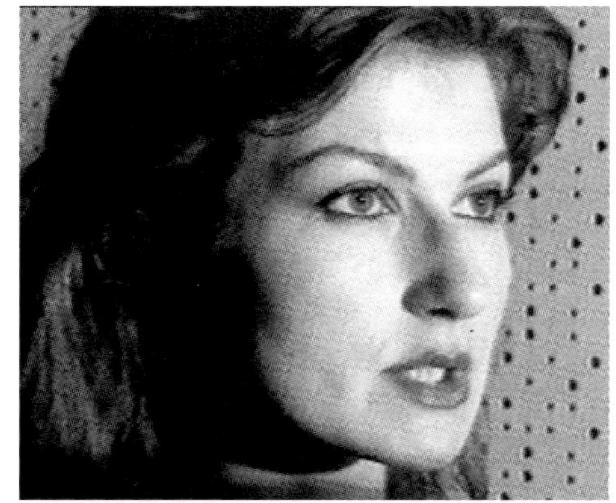

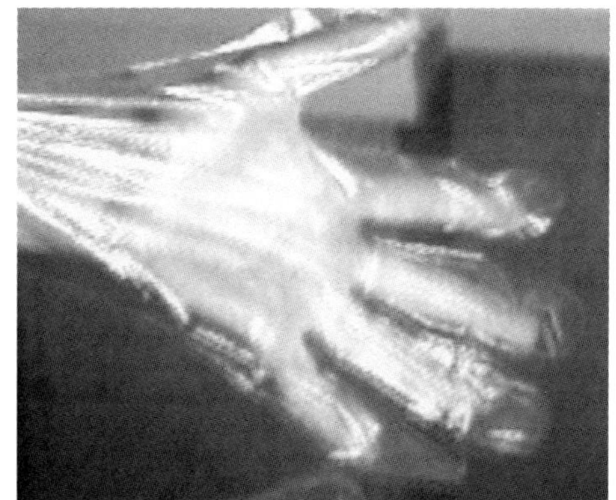

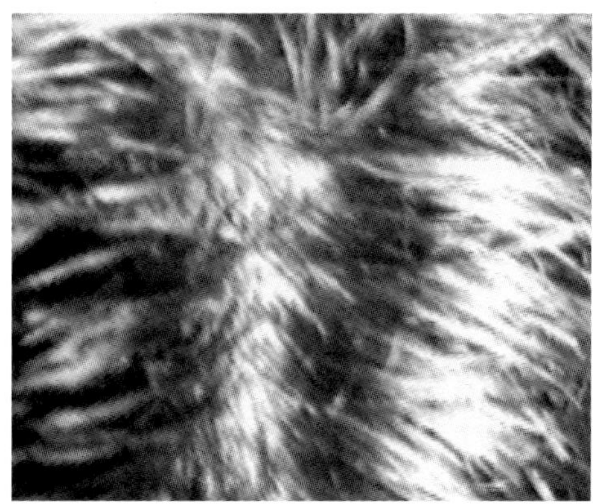

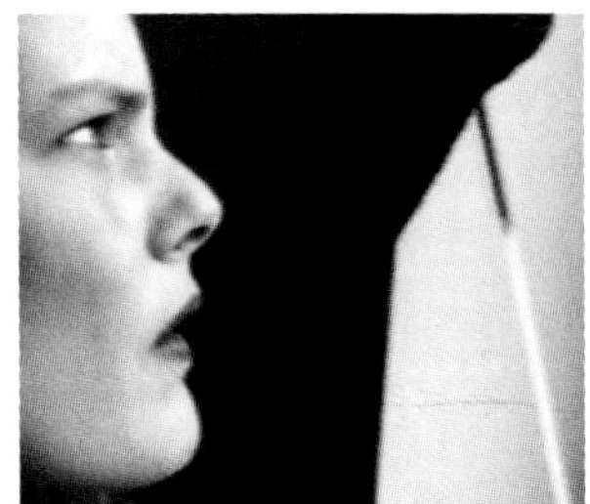

Can I come over?
I'm afraid not.
I thought you'd be…
Have you managed to do everything you wanted to?
No.
I left you.
I know.
Is it something I…
You couldn't…
What's the matter with?
Nothing. Everything is just fine.
I bought something.
Yep.
I saw the most.
You did?
Got one even for you.
Good.
That's really good.
That's more than good. That's fantastic.

Sissy used to excite me, like kind of used to thrill me, fascinate me. Those amazing unbelievable stories she had. She'd purchase them of course, everything she could she would, but what a fag, the things she'd come up with, how stimulating it was, a remarkable feedback one got from her. How inspiring, I could listen to her for hours!

Sissy was brought to me void. For sometime someone has been trying to revive her. I had very little faith in that. You've got to be a complete fool to let yourself go with it and Sissy was far too educated to gain any benefit out of it.
Must remember: Sissy was a dear, an expert on so many things, she wouldn't miss a word you'd tell her, but couldn't make a thing out of it, not for herself anyway.
A barren human being. I used to say, "Come to terms with yourself." She never could. It was extremely easy for me then. I'd bring her in public where she could hold any conversation. We'd go home. I'd correct her. She'd shout. I'd do it anyway, quietly but surely I'd fist her. She'd ask, "Please say something nice to me." I'd tell her how big and strong her back was and what a swimmer she could make, after which I'd fall asleep.

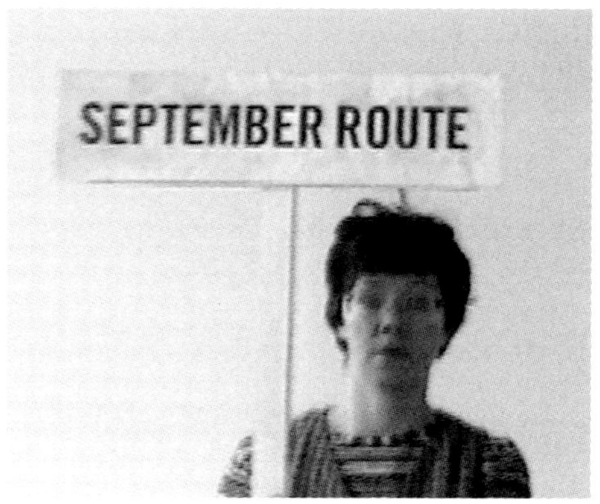
SEPTEMBER ROUTE

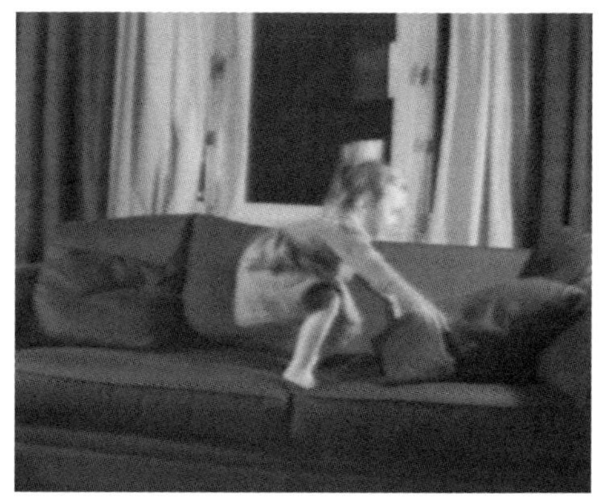

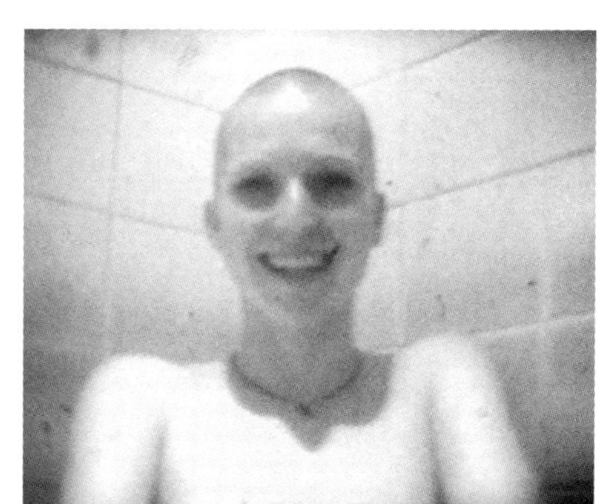

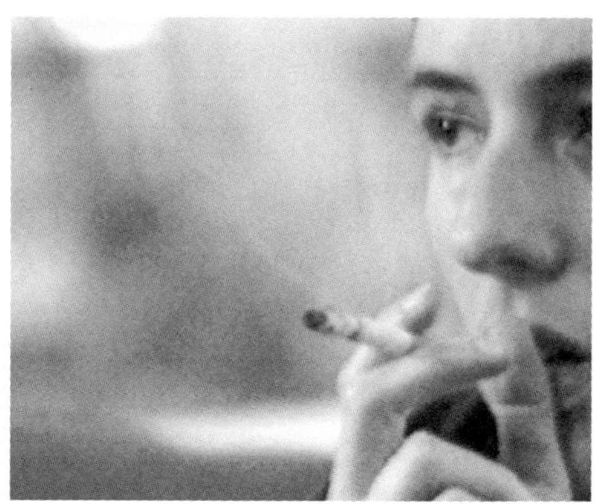

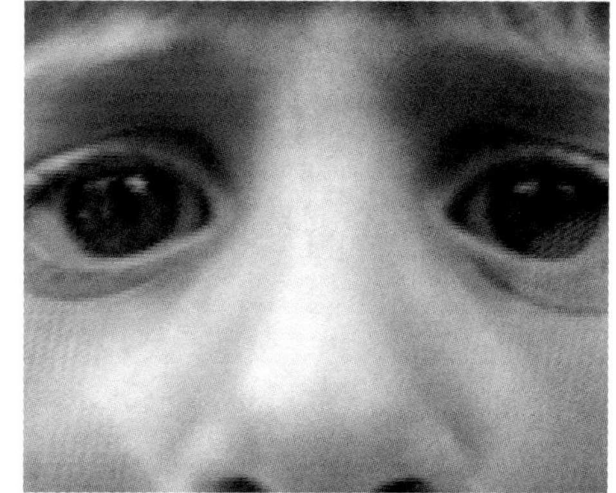

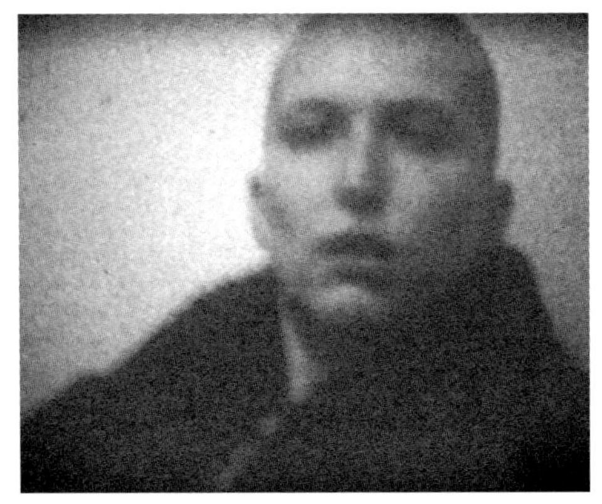

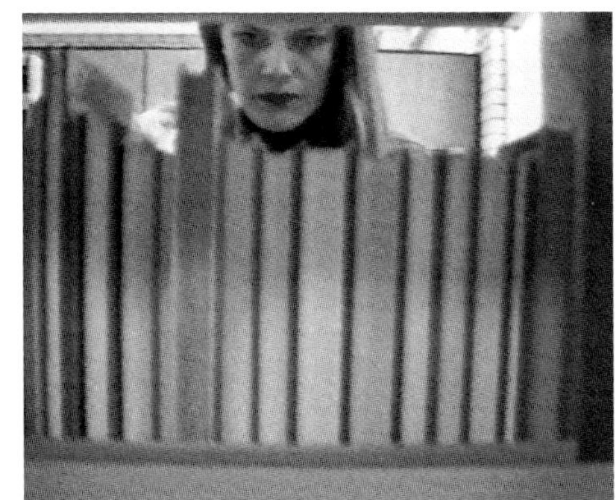

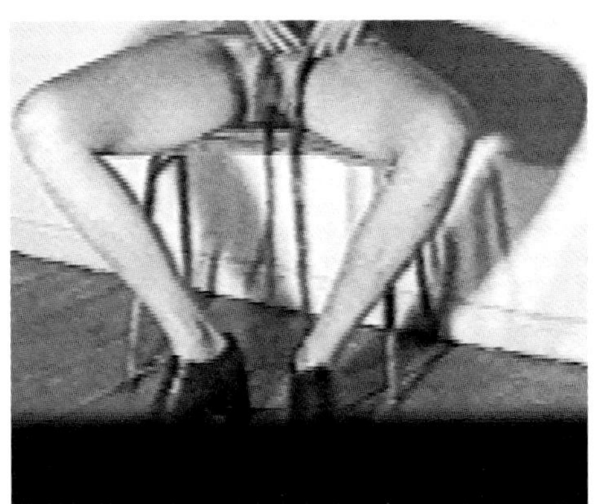

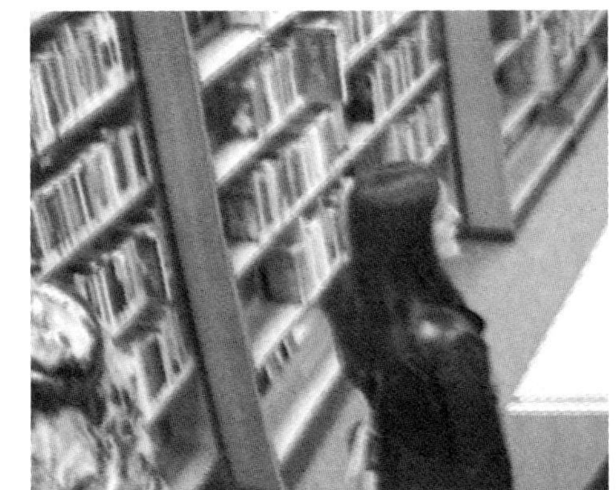

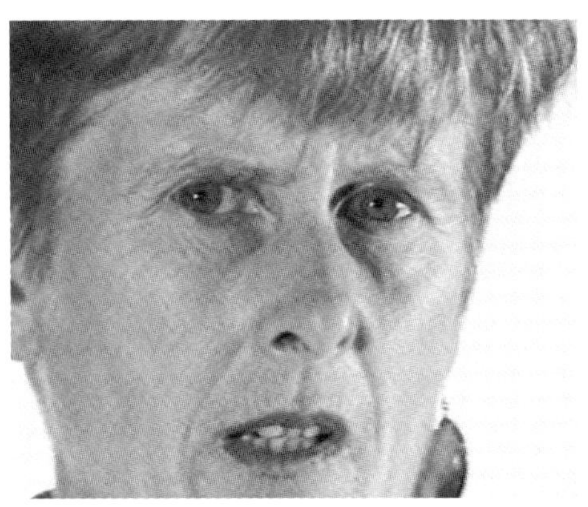

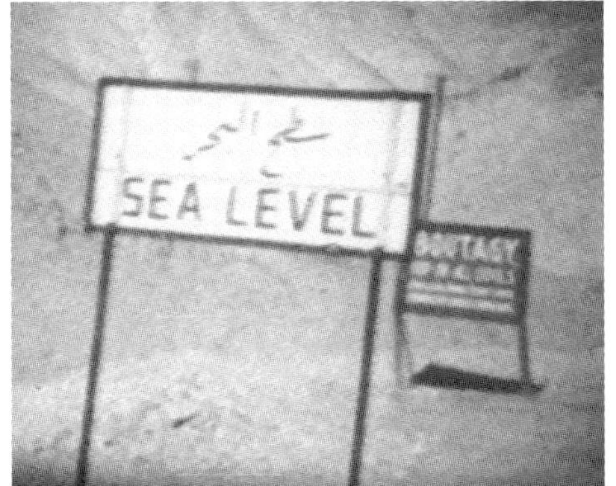
SEA LEVEL

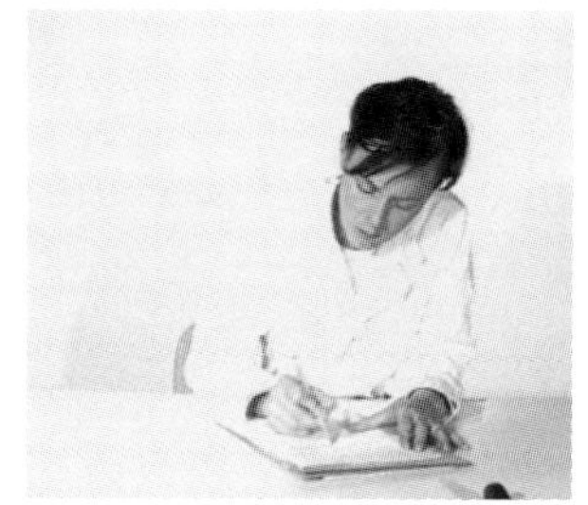

Sissy won't let me sleep. I'm holding my eyelids wide open as if I'm a corpse. Sissy won't mind talking to a corpse. As a corpse, I somehow do mind. I'm humiliating myself as a corpse, asking her to go. Sissy can't handle my humiliated carcass. She weeps and promises not to leave me alone. I won't be a swimmer in a million years, neither will she.

So Sissy was trying to find me in bookshops. She piled them up around her bed and slept among them. I sleep with my books. Sissy though, never fucked a book in her life (something I always found bizarre). She could y'know masturbate on them. She'd tenderly caress purple, hard covers, she'd feel the imprint, she'd softly sprint over pages, she'd smell them, she'd even scrub their spines, but couldn't fuck 'em. Never! Always incapable. (I've tried to plant some hope in her. But y'know there's no hope in teaching such things.) A book cover could easily remind her of me, so she says. A series, two volumes in a cardboard box, a bilingual edition of something I'd never buy, could give her the kick; limited editions, collector's freshly squeezed. All she'd purchase I'm all over.

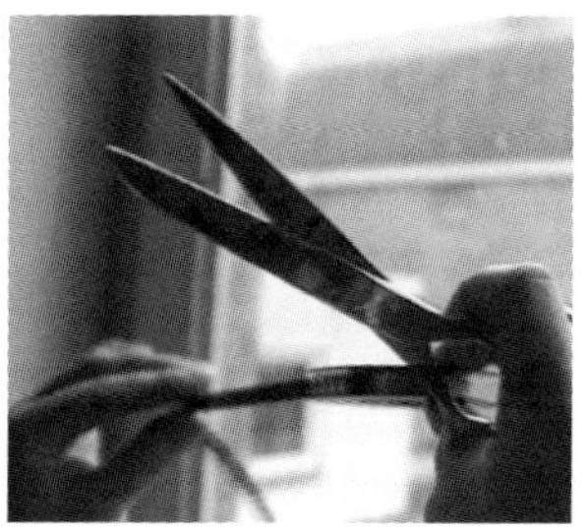

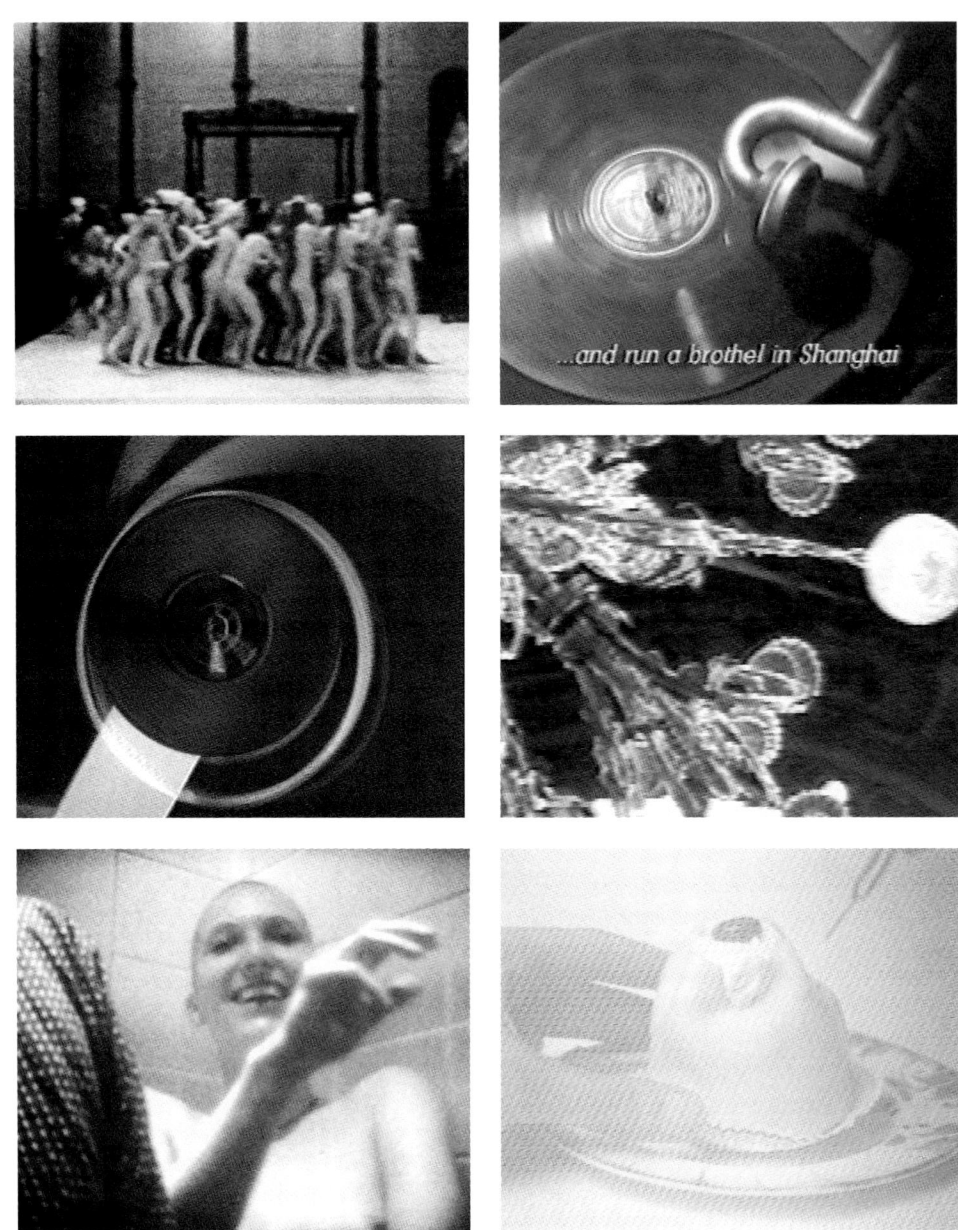
...and run a brothel in Shanghai

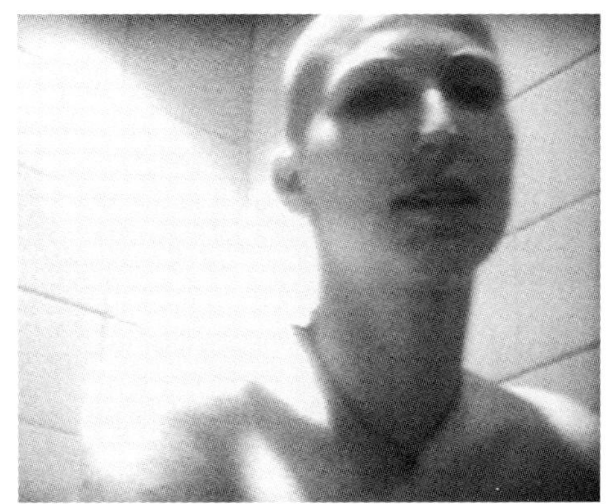

Then I'd run in again and Sissy was waiting. And then she was getting her tantrums. She knew I couldn't help enjoying them, they were the only occasions she had. Show-time. I stirred them up for her. On stage Sissy started playing those tantrums for me. I was everything. I became the healer. Where the pseudo-revivers could never reach ~ he could. When ego was lost ~ he was. What Western education couldn't become ~ he became. I stayed and I came. Sissy would come into her tantrums and Septembers would become welcoming for tantrums. Everybody lived ever after.

Oh, dear Sissy I've missed you so, I would say when I came. Sissy would grin then, her colourless hair would fall on her grin, she'd chew it and suck it and it would stick to her cheeks and it would get between your teeth and it'll be everywhere, jammed to my toes and all over her thighs and sticky and long and some short and you'll never be able to be without Sissy ever again, she'd be all over you and you'd die.

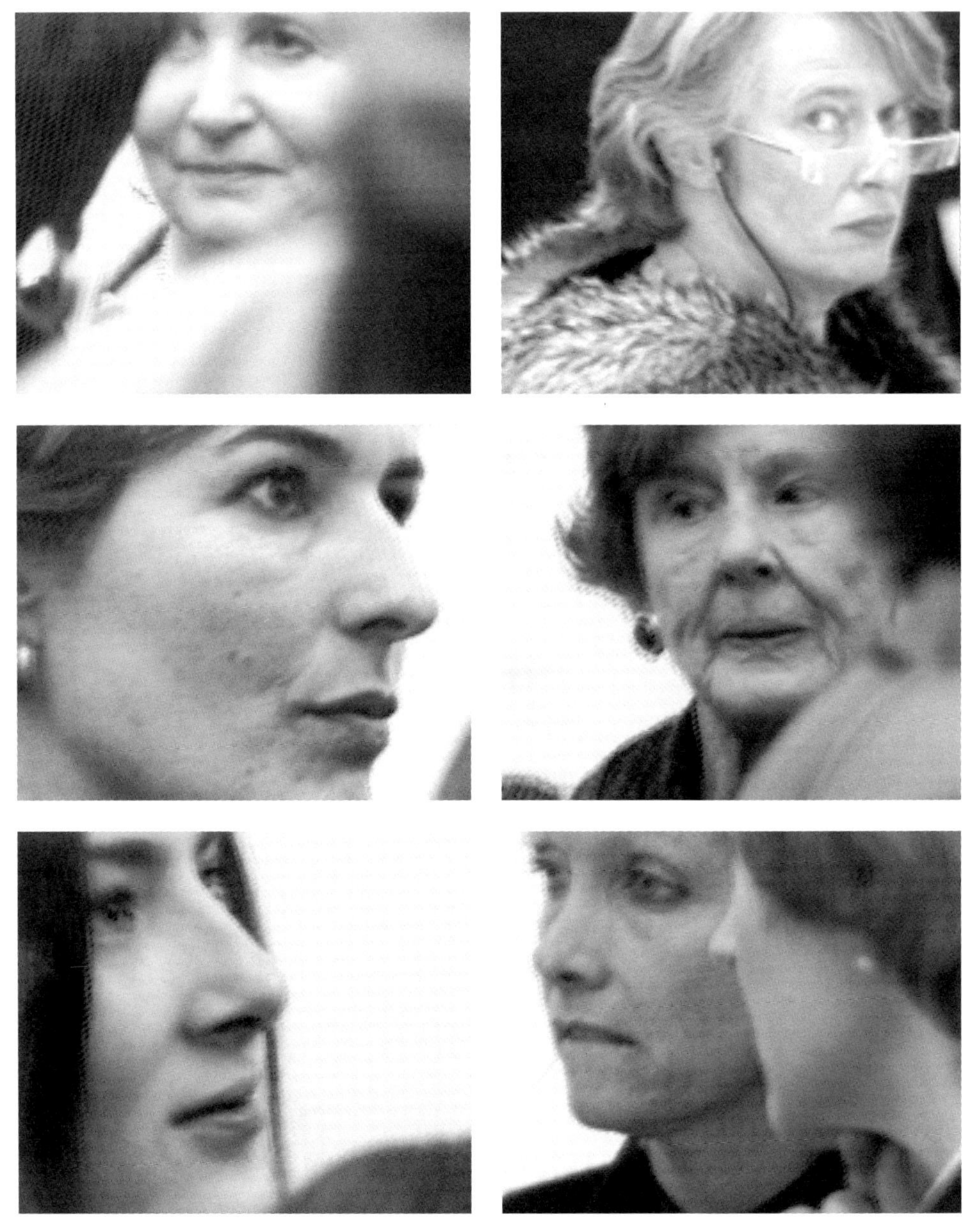

I immediately imagined a long September. Every time I saw her I'd plan another September. It got to the point when I would have had twelve Septembers in mind, planned in detail, every time before I came to see her. Then she'd be more beautiful than ever.

das pelzchen

Critic	I know when an art work is lying, always!
Woman	It reminds me of everything I want to forget.
Guide	Please concentrate. A blow-up detail.
Man	No, it's not at all cruel!
Security	Okay. That's it.
Voice	I don't want you to call me again.
Man	Me to surprise you as a marvellous painting.
Song	Once I loved and I gave so much love to this love.

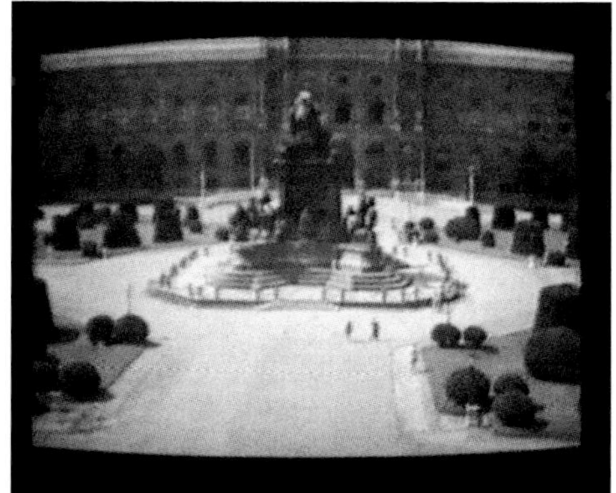

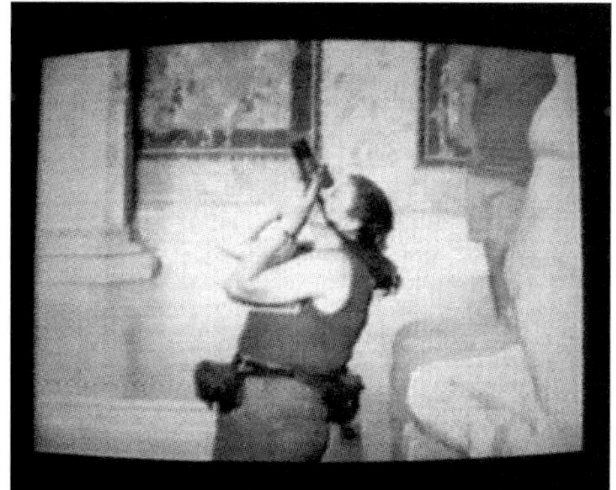

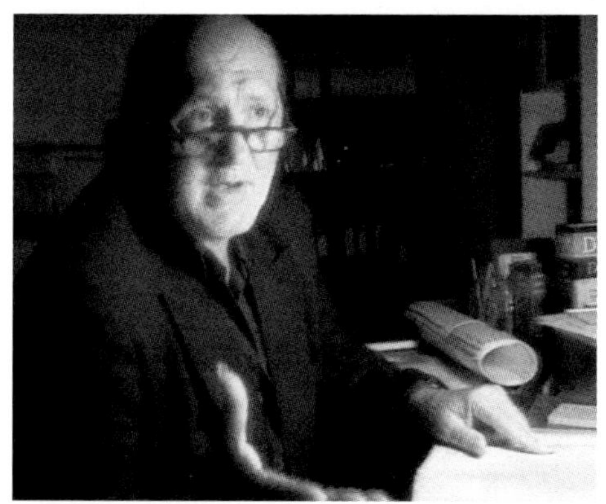

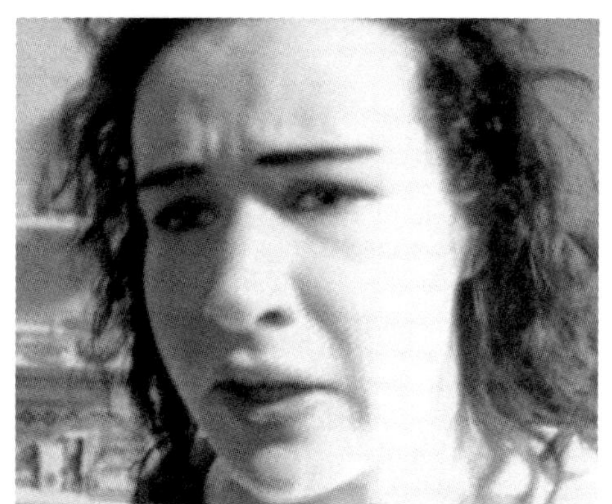

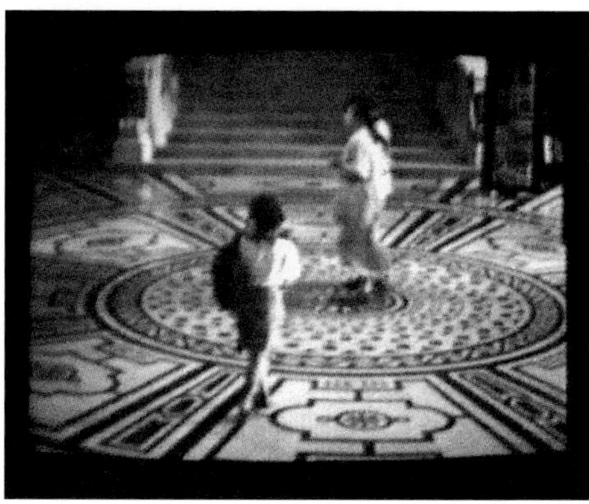

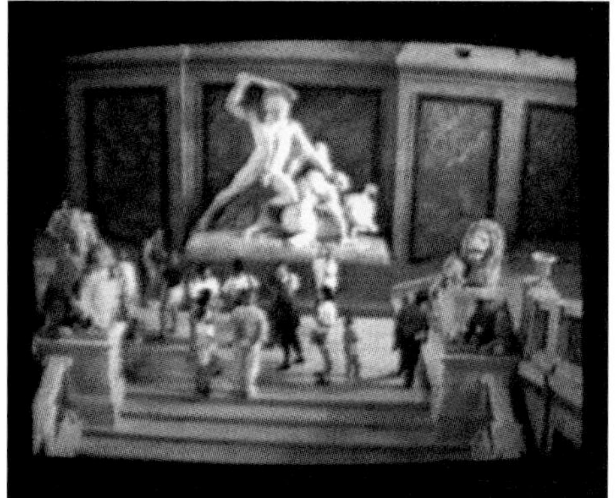

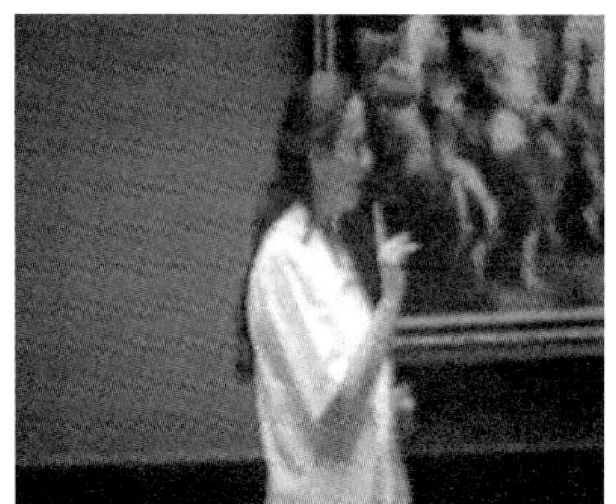
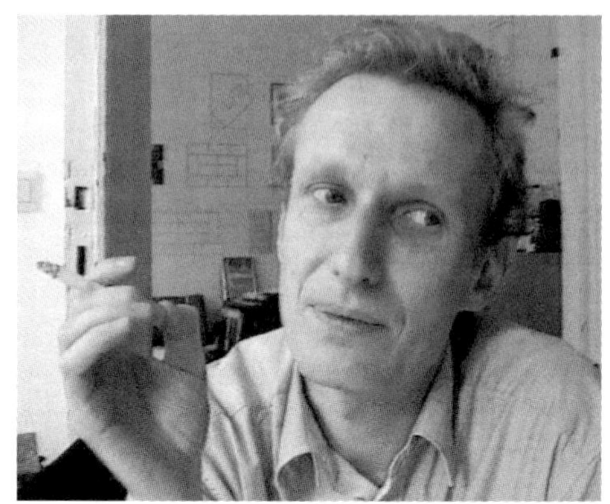
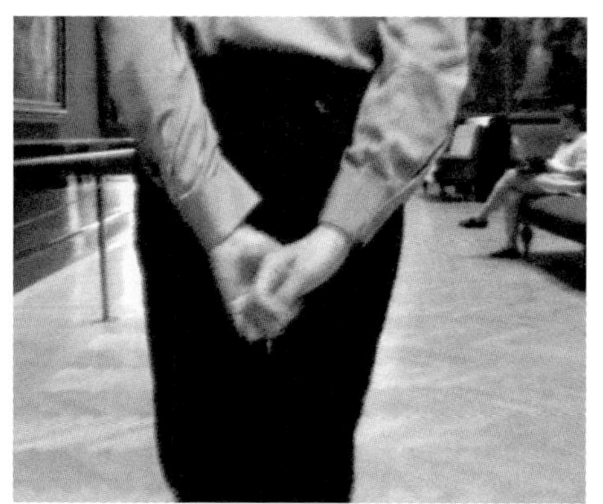
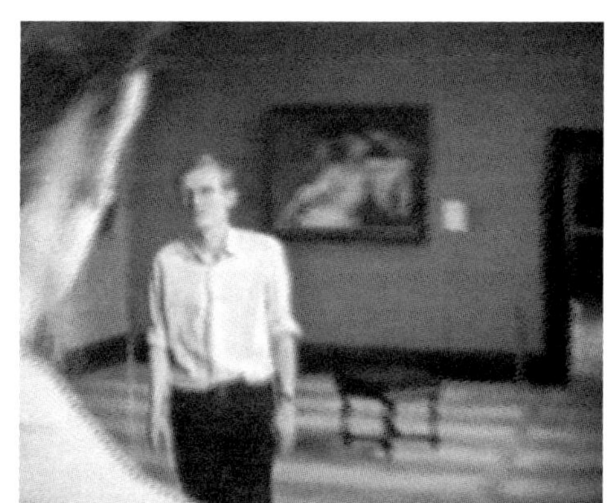
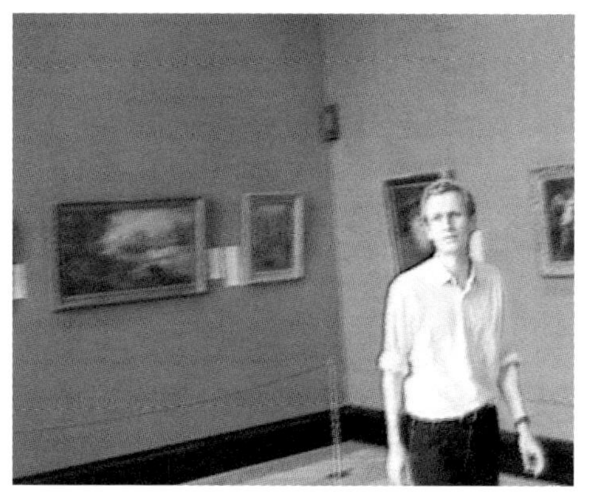
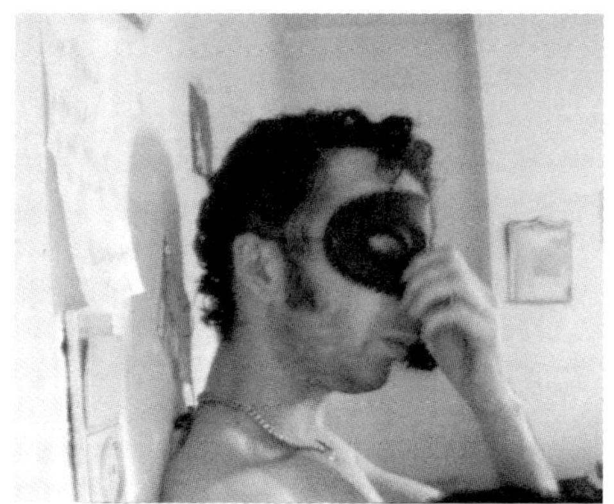

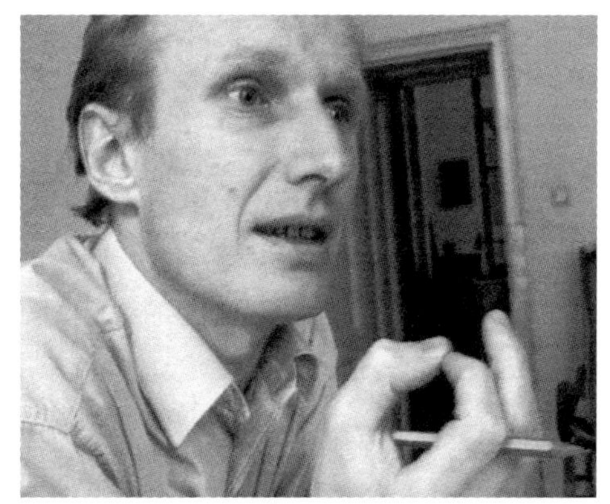

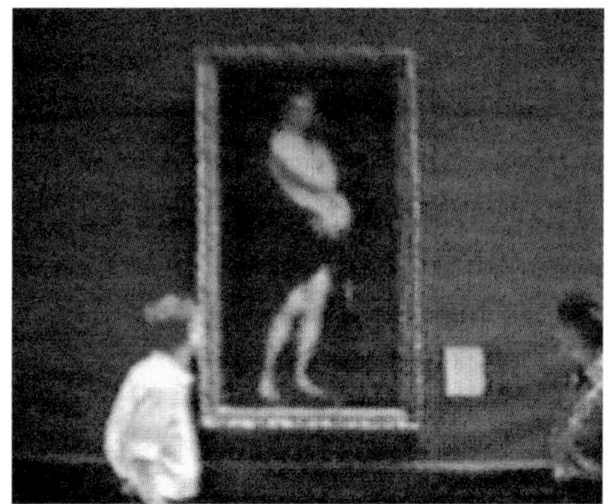

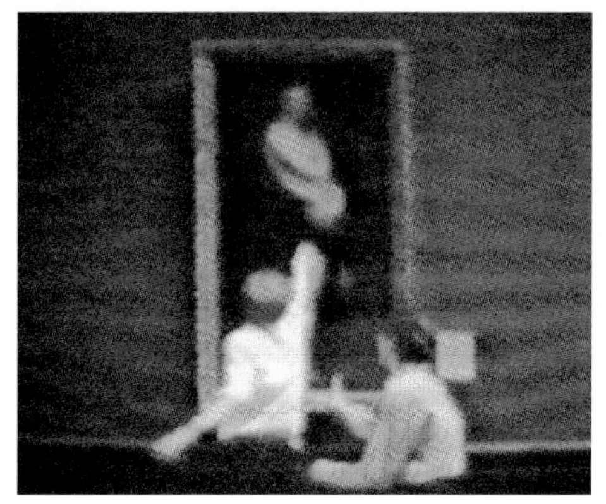

*footnote

This book is in the middle of the river at Koptos, in an iron box.
In the iron box is a bronze box.
In the bronze box is a sycamore box.
In the sycamore box is an ivory and ebony box.
In the ivory and ebony box is a silver box.
In the silver box is a golden box and in that is the book.
It is twisted all round with snakes and scorpions and all other
crawling things and there is a deathless snake by the box.

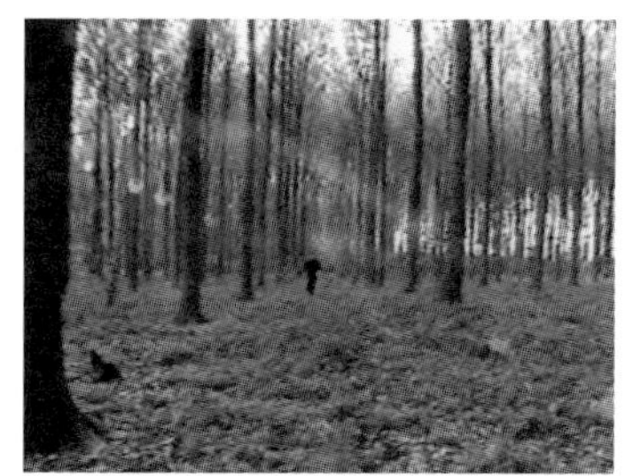

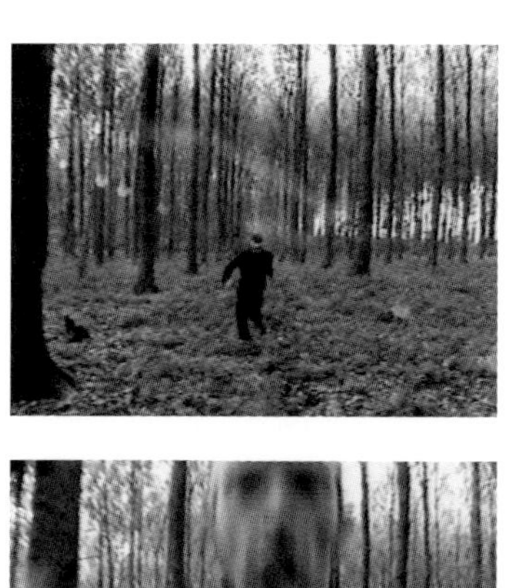

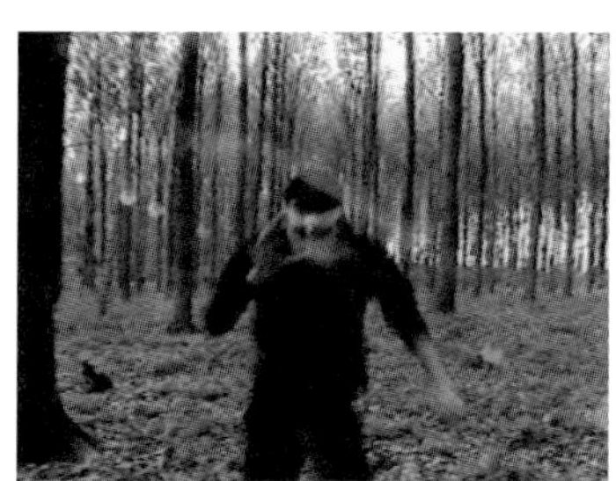

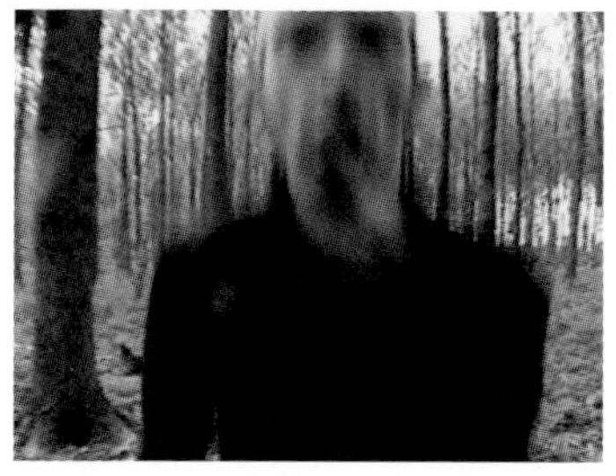

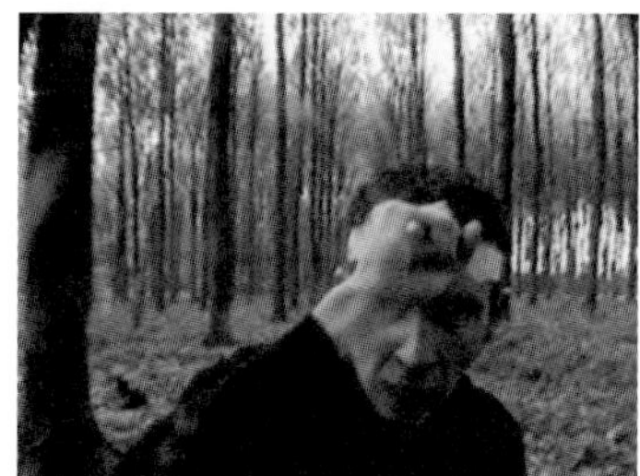

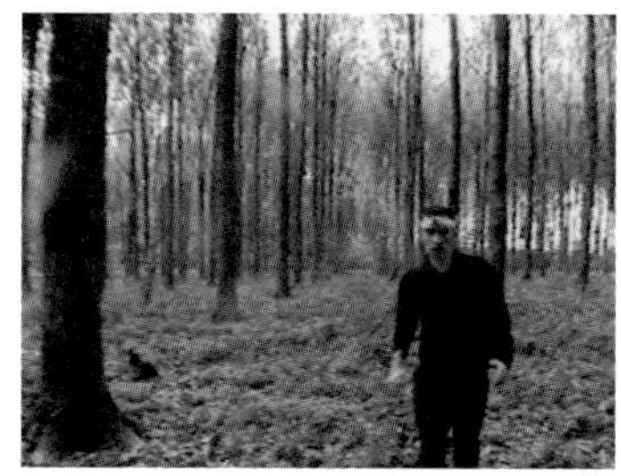

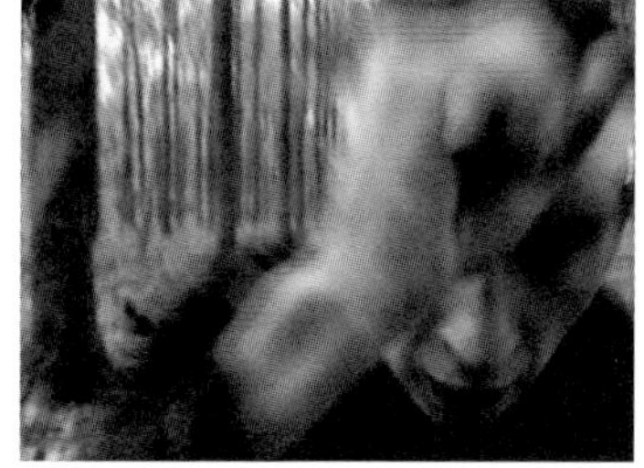

natalya

First Story:
which concerns itself with a broken mirror and what happened to its fragments.

Second Story:
which is about a little boy and a little girl.

Third Story:
the flower garden of the old woman who knew magic.

Fourth Story:
in which appear a prince and princess.

Fifth Story:
which is about the robber girl.

Sixth Story:
the Lapp woman and the Finnish woman.

Seventh Story:
what happened in the Snow Queen's palace and afterwards.

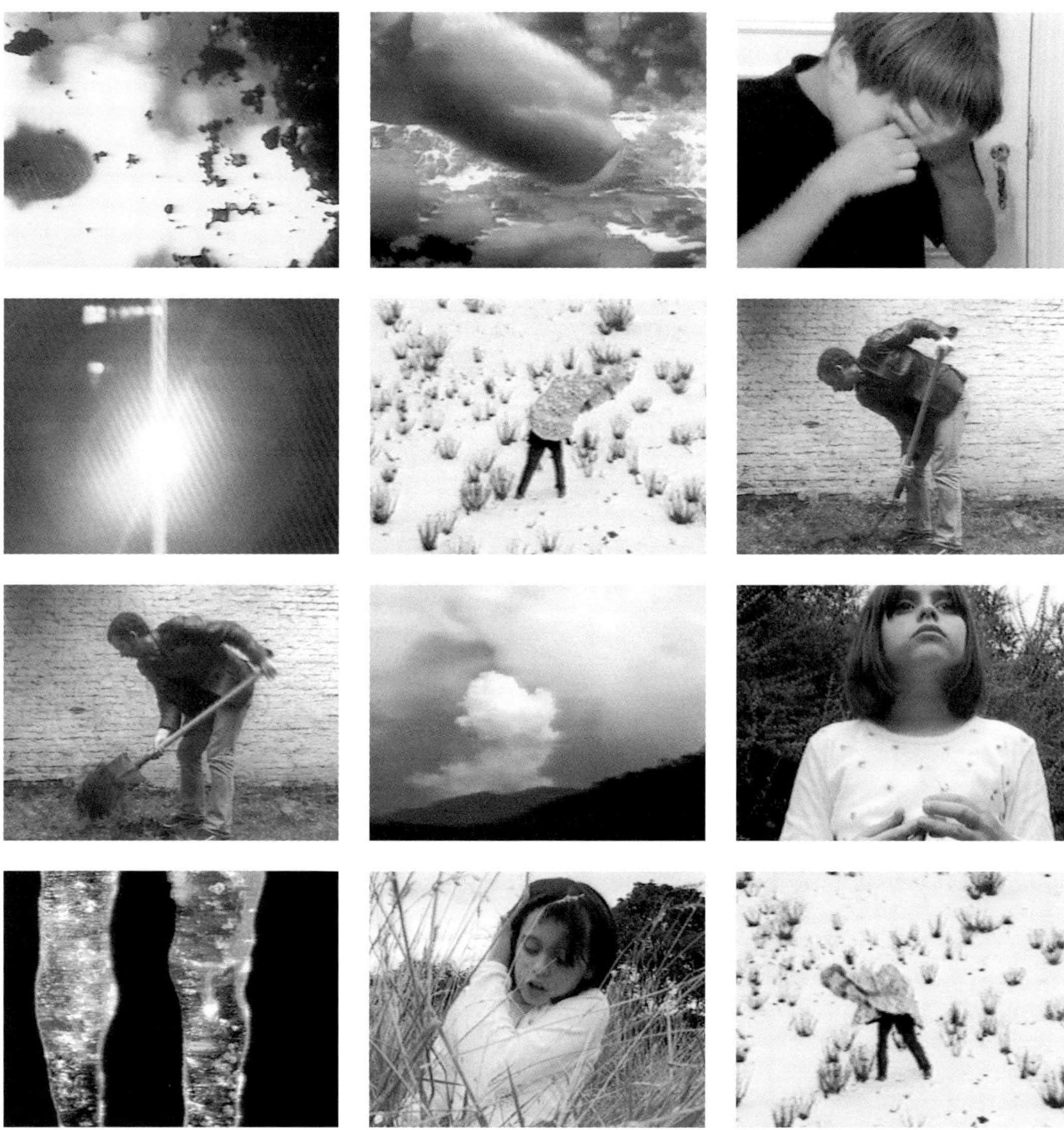

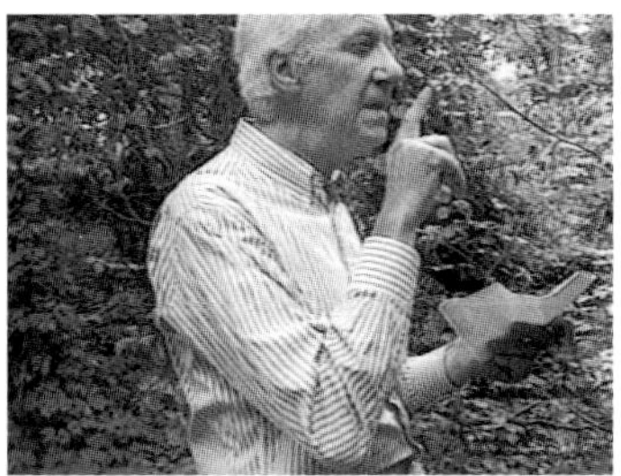

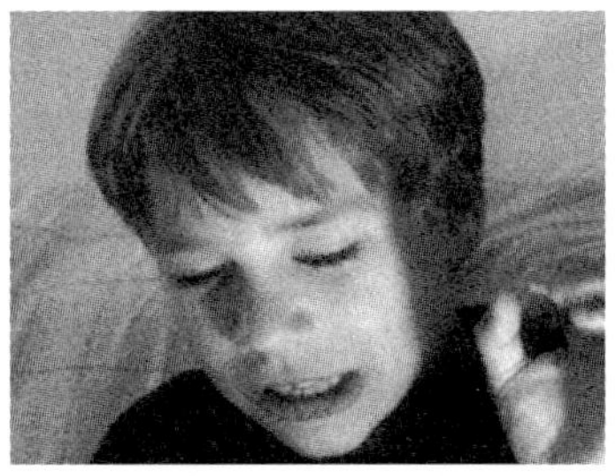

Cirrostratus, cirrocumulus, altocumulus, altostratus, nimbostratus, stratocumulus, cumulus, cumulonimbus.

I can see the sky, filled with dust, like the cone of air, crossed by the rays of a projector in a theatre auditorium.

I'm really happy because I've invented this mirror that can show the inner look inside of all the people.

Imagine it then multiplied a thousand, billion times.

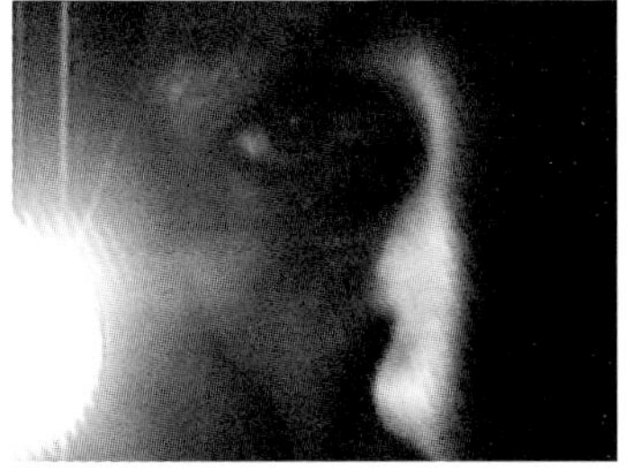

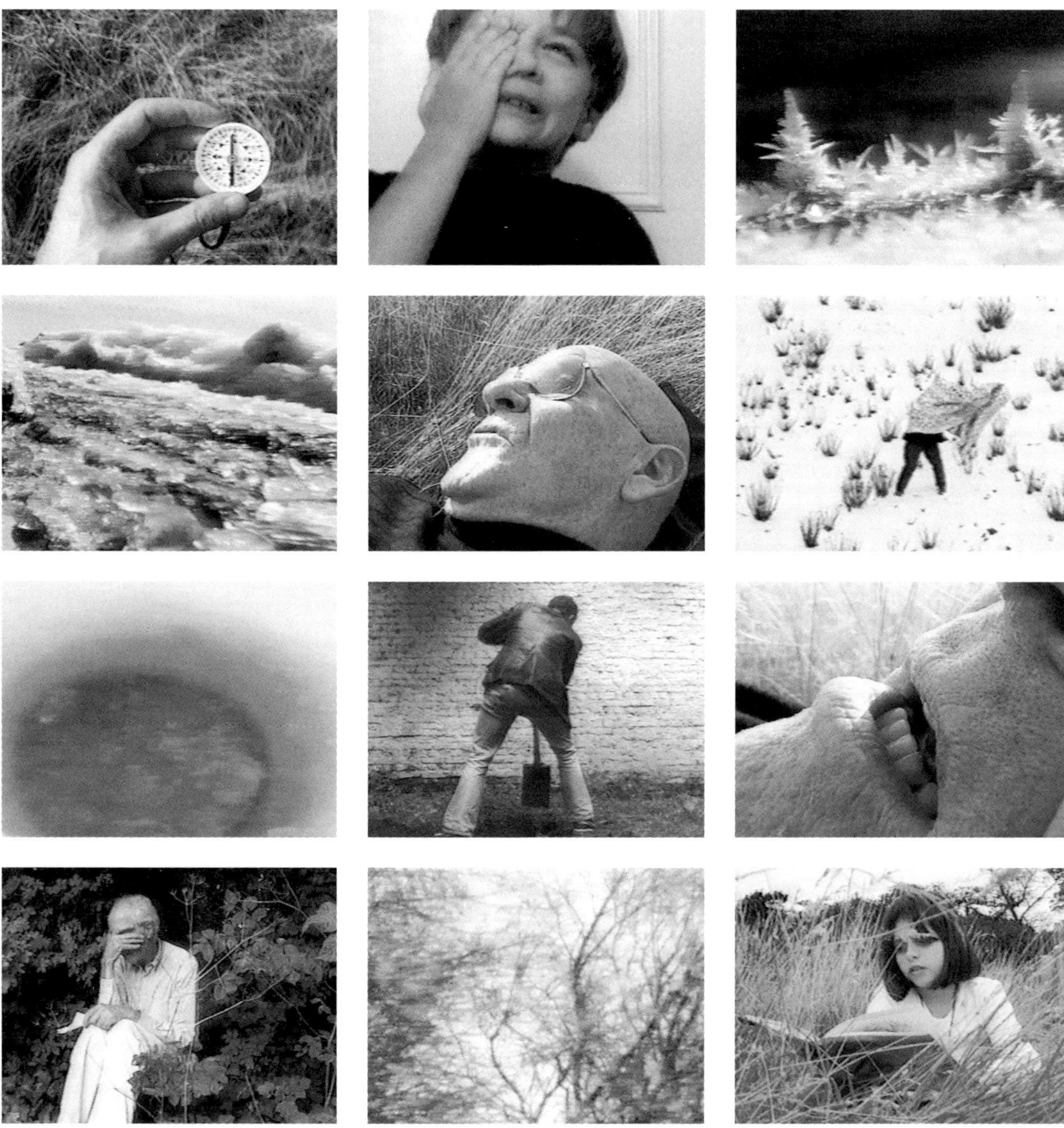

love in a cold climate

In answer to your request for help with information about 'The Snow Queen', we can tell you: the film was made more than 30 years ago, and many of those involved in its creation have not survived until the present day.
(LARGELY ILLEGIBLE) Natalya Klimova was born in 1938. In 1962 she graduated from the Moscow Arts Theatre School of Drama, in the mid-sixties she was an actress at the Modern Theatre. At Lenfilm she played Ada in 'Into the Storm', 1965; 'The Snow Queen', 1966; Efimia in 'First Russians', 1967; Spring in 'Snowmaiden', 1968.

We know nothing of her further history.

Уважаемый господин Кьюрэн!

В ответ на Вашу просьбу помочь Вам в сборе материалов о фильме «Снежная королева» можем сообщить следующее:
Фильм снимался свыше 30 лет назад, и многие из его создателей не дожили до наших дней. Из основных авторов фильма остался лишь

Об основных актерах Вы можете прочитать в энциклопедическом кинословаре, изданном в Москве в 1986г.
Наталья Климова родилась в 1938 году, окончила школу-студию при МХАТ им. Горького в 1962 г., в середине 60-х годов – актриса театра «Современник». На студии «Ленфильм» снималась в фильмах: «Иду на грозу» (1965, Ада), «Снежная королева» (1966, Снежная королева), «Первороссияне» (1967, Ефимия), «Снегурочка» (1968, Весна).
О дальнейшей судьбе актрисы нам ничего не известно.

С уважением,

Иванеев Дмитрий Георгиевич
(музей и информационный отдел киностудии «Ленфильм.)

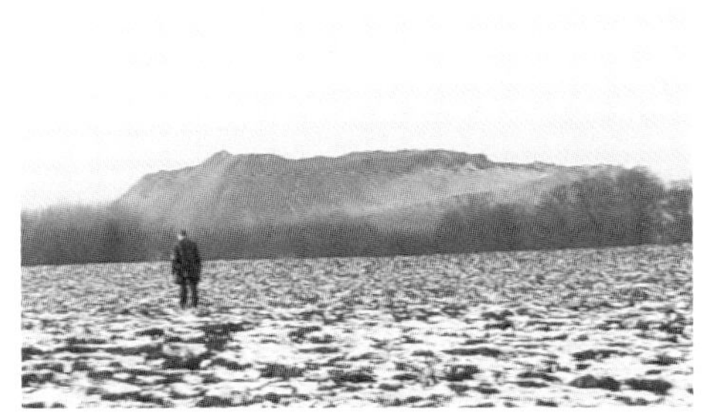

And there's love… there's love that hurts… there's love with pain and there's all these different turns of the kaleidoscope – all these different sort of takes on it. And then there's blind love.

Don't go kissin' by the garden gate!
'cos love is blind but the neighbours ain't!

When did you first fall in love?

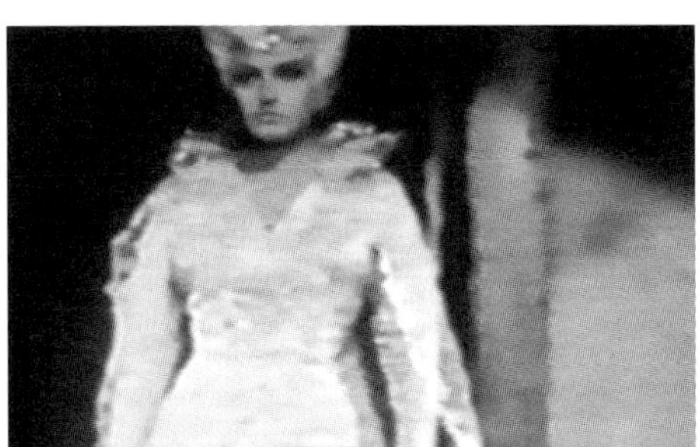

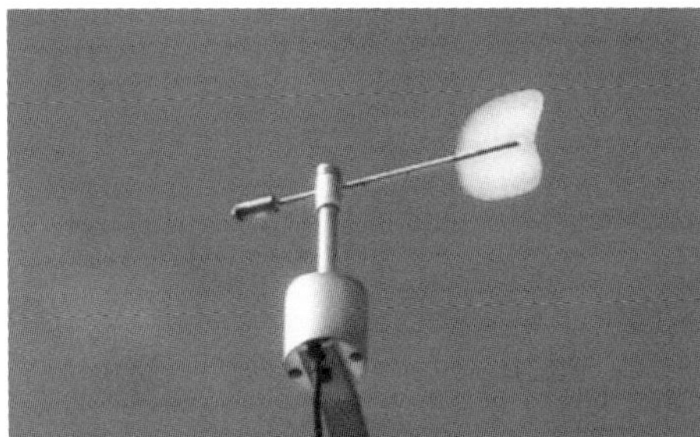

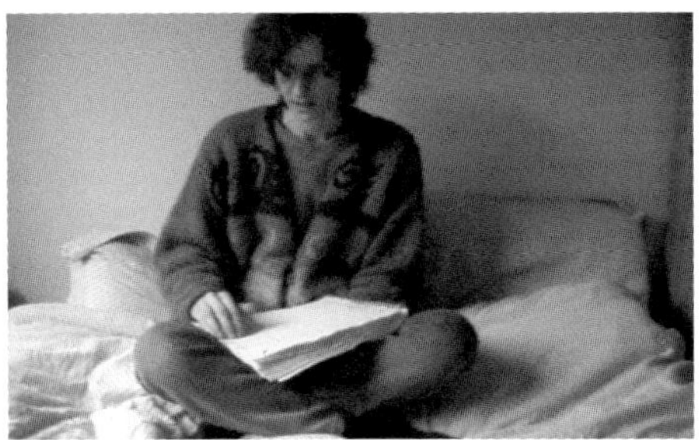

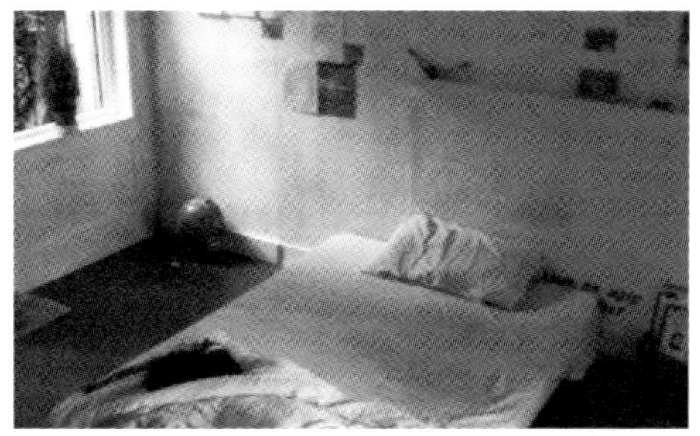

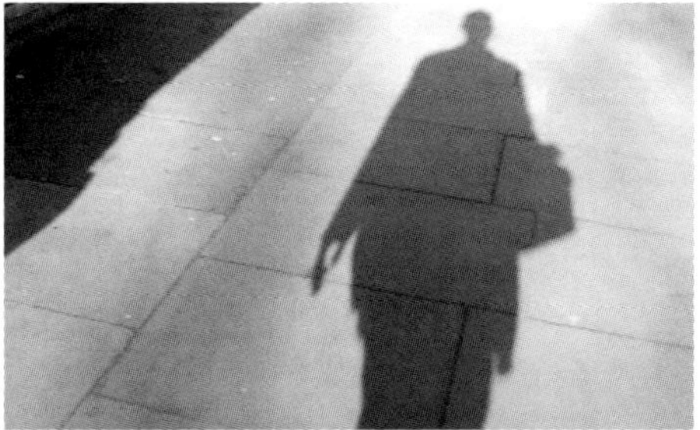

When a sliver like that entered someone's eye it stayed there; and the person, forever after, would see the world distorted and only be able to see the faults, and not the virtues, of everyone around him, since even the tiniest fragment contained all the evil qualities of the whole mirror.

If a splinter should enter someone's heart – oh, that was the most terrible of all – that heart would turn to ice.

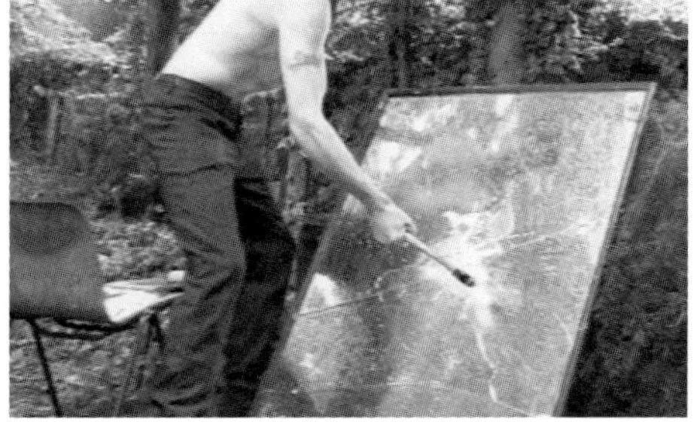

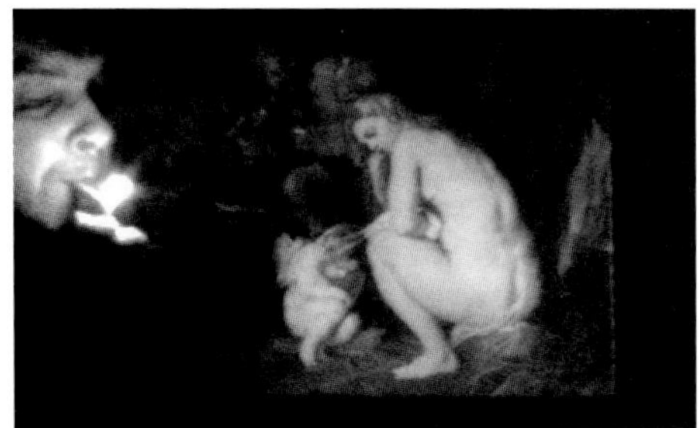

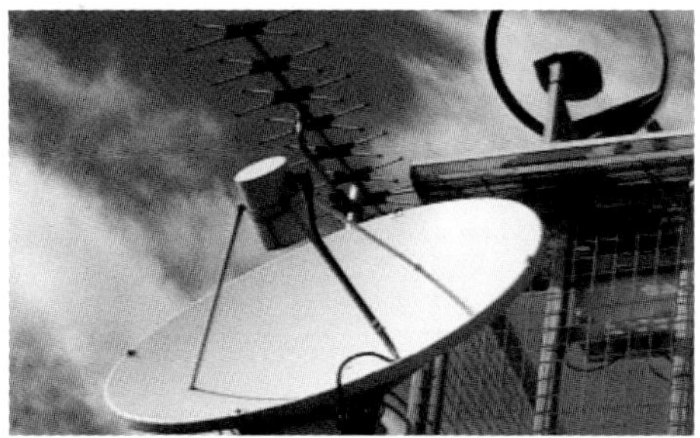

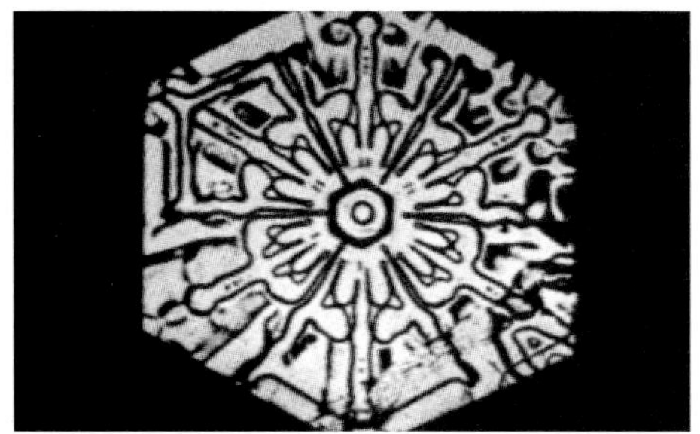

The snowflakes grew bigger and bigger until they looked like white hands that were running alongside him. At last the big sled stopped and its driver stood up and turned to look at him. The fur hat and coat were made of snow – the driver was a woman.

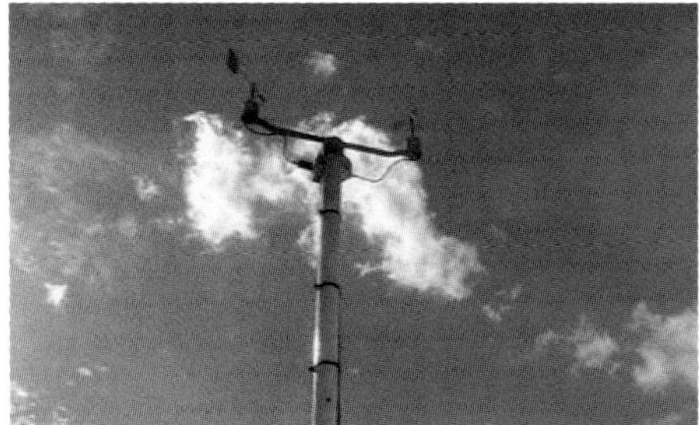

You're desperate for lifeform but to have a moment without lifeform makes you more aware of the first bird you see – the first sound of something else – or the first tree. So to take it away means that in the putting back it becomes quite heightened. I think it's the way it heightens all your senses by there gradually being less and less, until there's an infinity in the end by taking it all away.

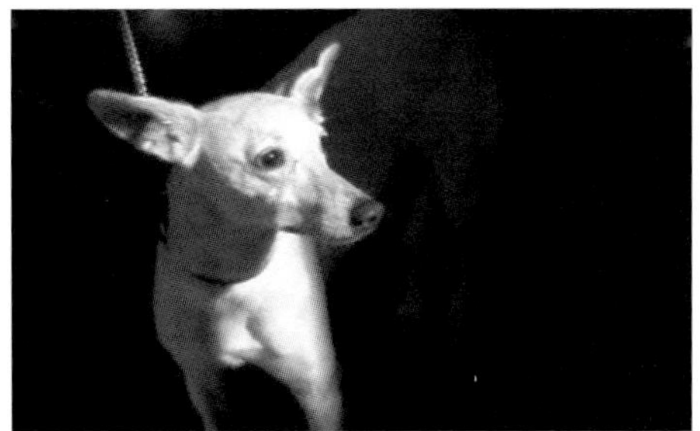

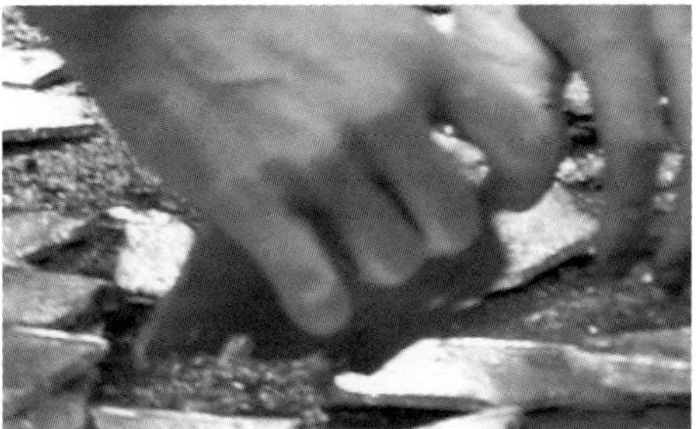

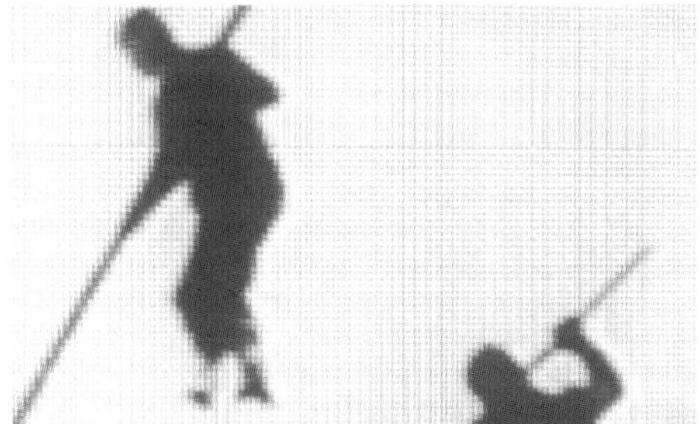

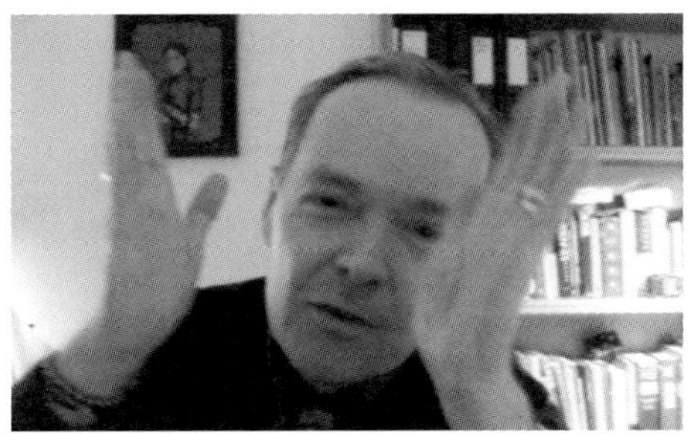

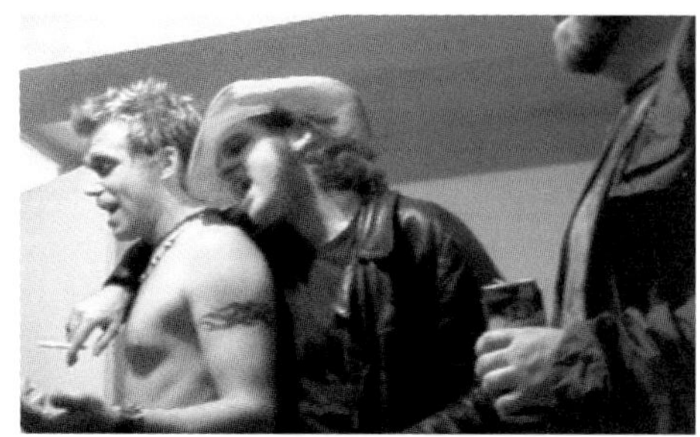

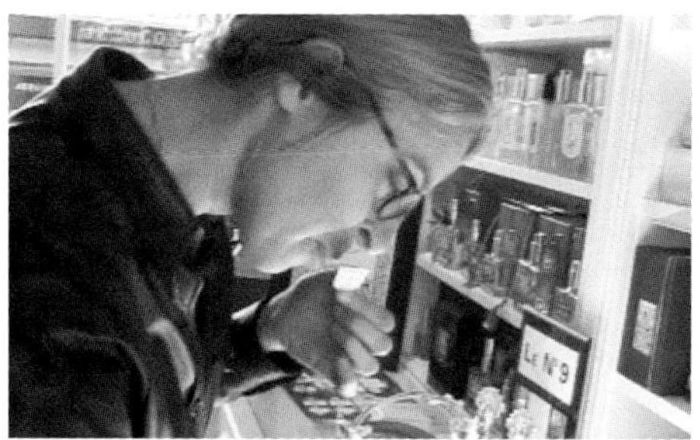

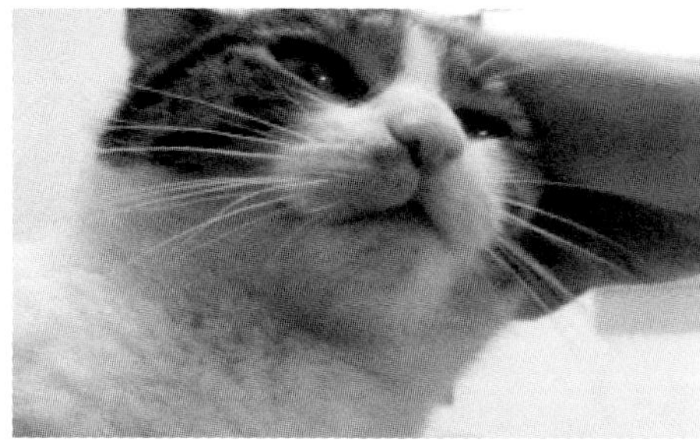

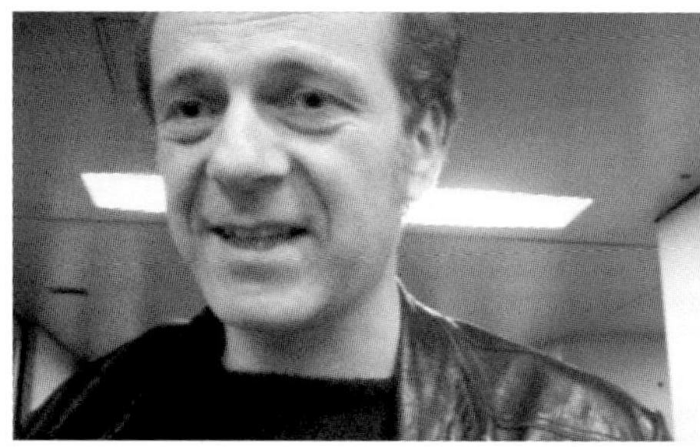

Well there's a whole lot in the middle!
It doesn't really end – it just peters out.
But I've forgotten the word for it...
It's called a damp ta ta ta.
It's not a cliffhanger – it's the opposite of that...

If the clouds rise and twist in different directions.

If the birds be silent.

If cattle run round and collect together in the meadows.

If birds of passage arrive early from colder climates.

If the cold increases whilst it snows, as soon as it begins to freeze.

If the wind blow north-east in winter.

If the ice cracks, expect the frost to continue.

If there be continued fogs.

If a snow-storm begins at a time when the moon is young, the rising of the moon will clear the snow away.

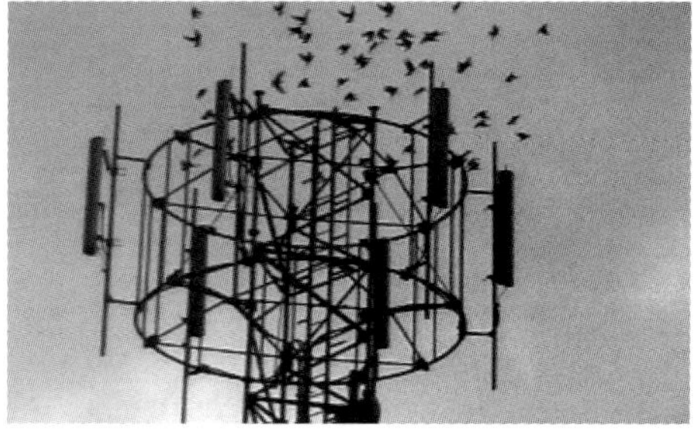

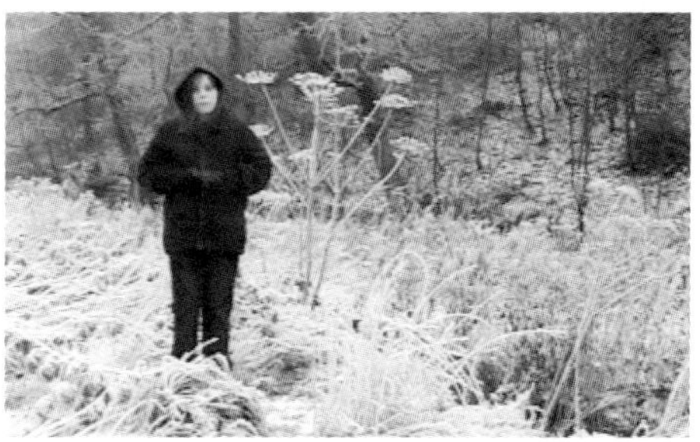

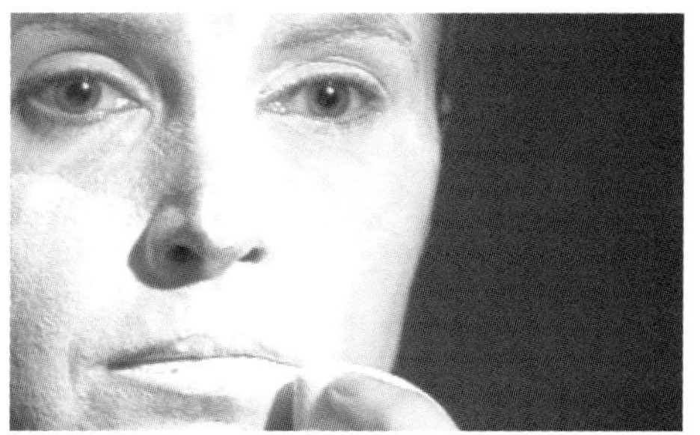

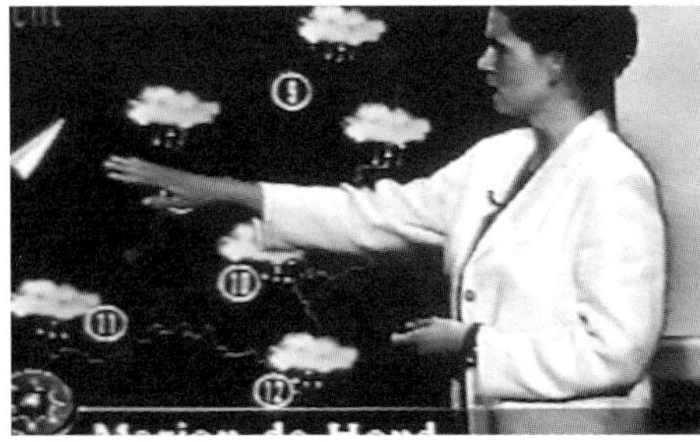

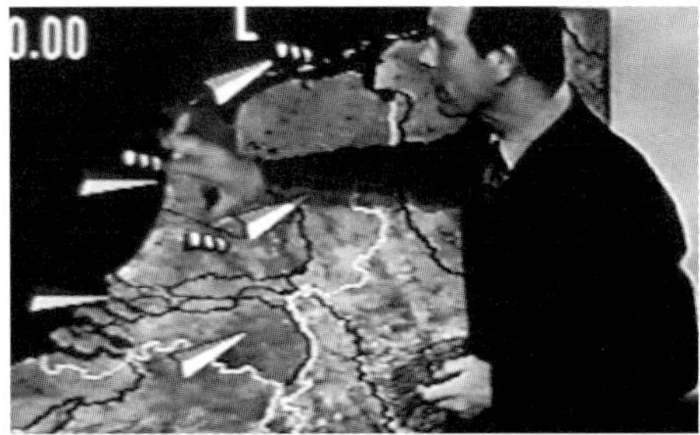

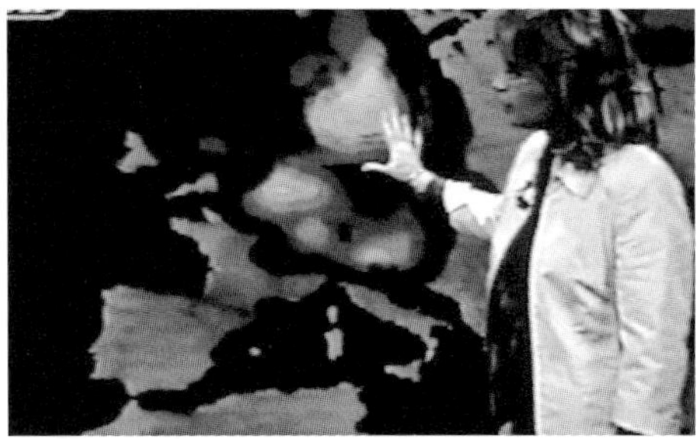

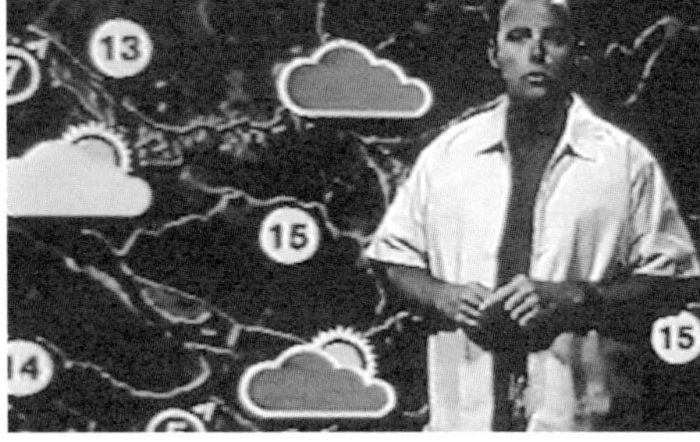

Camph	Extreme coldness of the surface to touch
Caps	Chill begins in back between shoulders
Carbo	Coldness with thirst
Cedron	At 6 pm; comes on with clock-like regularity
Cuprum	With cold sweat on forehead, contracted, irregular pulse
Dig	Coldness of hands and feet
Eup-pur	Chill in small of back, extending all over
Euph	Shivering all the time
Gels	Chill without thirst, in back with muscular soreness
Hep	Very sensitive to cold, coughs as soon as gets cold or into draught
Ign	Chill with thirst
Ipec	Short chill, preceded by much prostration
Mosch	Creeping chilliness, much worse in evening
Nat-mur	Chill followed by heat with great thirst
Nux-vom	External chilliness, internal heat
Nat-mur	Chilliness and shivering with blue nails on being uncovered
Phos	Chill extends downward, fever upwards
Plum	Stubbornly persistent coldness

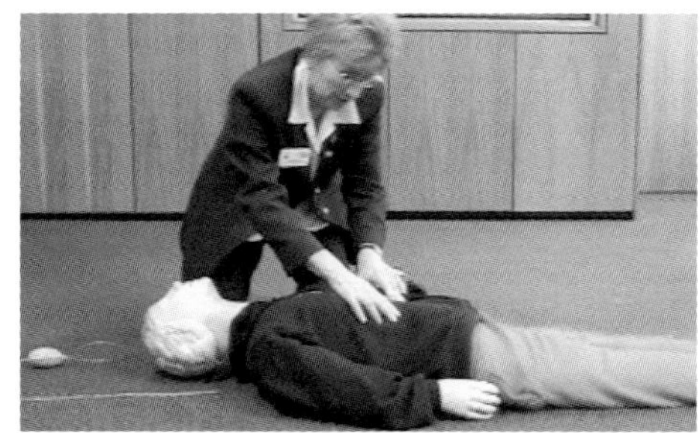

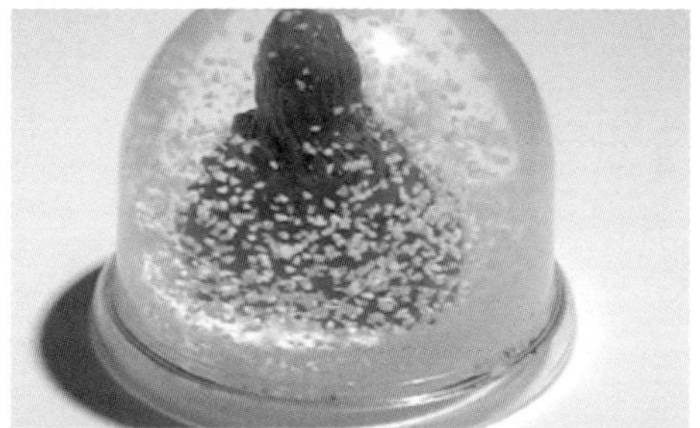

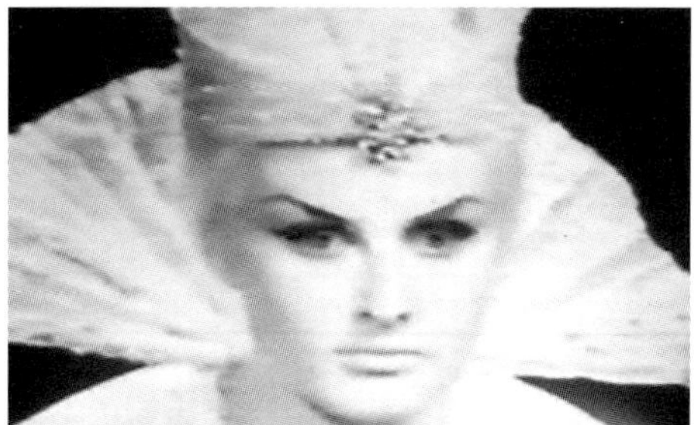

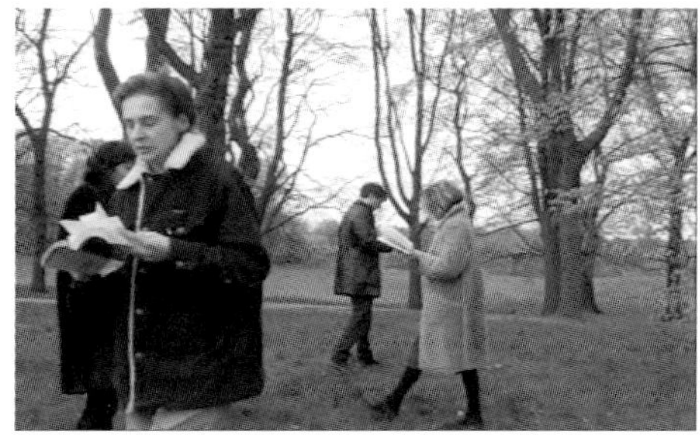

Coldness and the feeling of being cut off...
Solitude... it was after all a fairytale...
There were a few roles after that and then I stopped...
That was my history.

libidinal temporalities

jim mooney

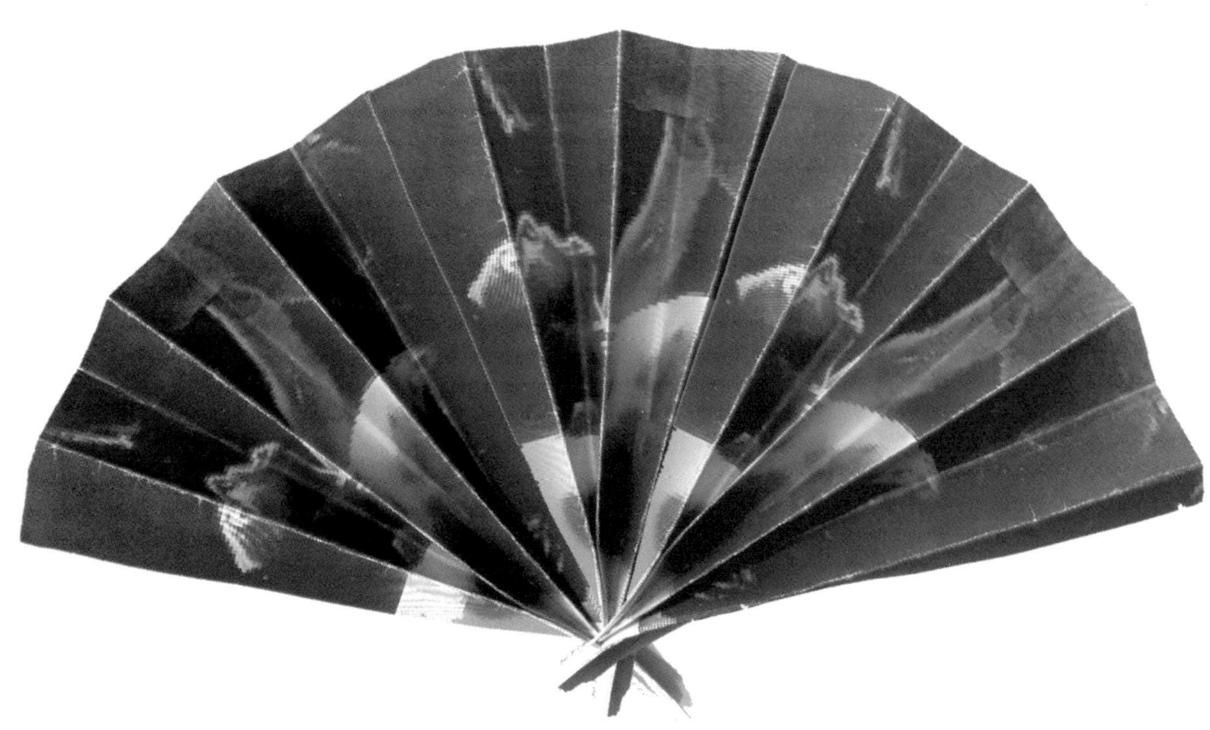

> The dialectic of joys and sorrows is never so absorbing as when it accords with the dialectic of time. We then know that it is time that takes and that gives. We suddenly become aware that time will take from us again.[1]

Time is among the most perplexing of all discursive subjects, and one from which I tend to shy away. However, in reviewing the range of Michael Curran's video work, time becomes the subject I can no longer side-step with any sense of impunity. This is not, I hasten to stress, due to the fact that video falls under that umbrella of practice known as time-based (a definition I have always felt owed its somewhat dubious provenance to the most impoverished reading of time as dull mechanistic duration). Rather, my interest in time here is prompted by the repeated reflection on time, and repetition in particular, which emerge as abiding concerns marking out the body of Curran's work.

When we begin to reflect upon time certain basic questions immediately arise and assume a pressing exigency. What is time? Can we know time? And, if so, how do we come to know time? When we talk of time, how can we be sure we talk of the same thing? How do we perceive the manifold shapes of time? Another way of posing this might be to ask: how is the invisible made visible? For, as we know, the invisible is no more and no less than the other face of the visible. Time is that invisible force which gives shape to the ever-changing, polymorphous face of the visible. We must not, however, expect to experience time as a homogeneous dimension; rather, we exist in different temporalities, experience different registers and speeds of duration simultaneously, confusingly and seemingly paradoxically. Not only do we experience the bewildering co-existence of different time scales, but we think in different metaphors of duration, and we most usually find ourselves enmeshed in ever fluctuating subjective and affective temporalities. Our awareness of these differing temporalities and durations may well be most keenly felt when we encounter them as presented in the form of the artwork. It is the artful artifice of the work of art, be it film, novel or painting, which is most capable of making conspicuous this bringing together of the dialectic of joys and sorrows with the dialectic of time. Otherwise, time is notoriously elusive, and yet, beguilingly, infuriatingly, determines our lives from the nothingness which precedes the beginning to the nothingness which follows on from the end and bestows upon us the exact duration of the intervening temporal span. We are inescapably in and of time; it is both our most intimate relation and the adversary we most fear. It shapes and destroys us, it breathes life into our lives and determines the very instant of our last gasp.

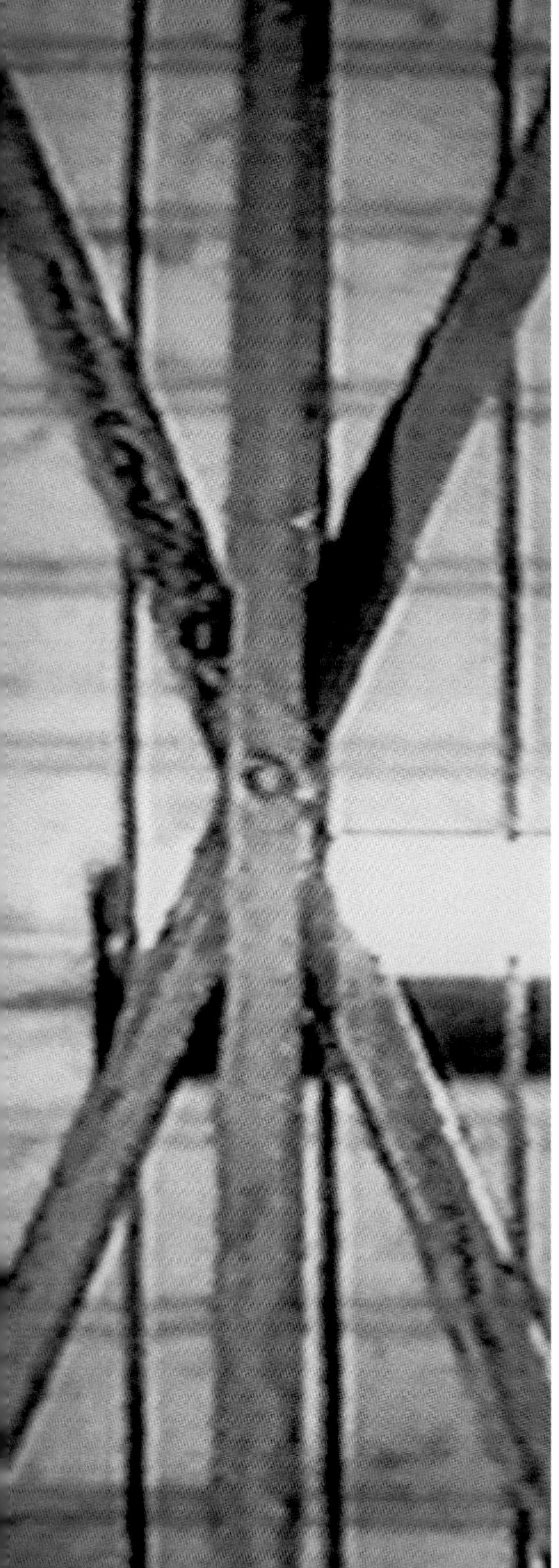

It must even by now be apparent that I think of meaningful time as being inextricably bound up with Being and, as such, far removed from the regulating measures we deploy to record its passing and its coming. We have no guarantee of the reassuring uniformity of time's continuity; indeed, this very intermingling of time and Being rather guarantees that our experience of time and the time of our experience contaminate and collude to dispel any illusion we might previously have held of the possibility of experiencing time as pure time.

This pure time would be the larger field of the time of the Other; what we might call, following on from the philosopher Gilles Deleuze, the groundless time of Thanatos. Time, in this sense, can only ever be what we know it to be as lived time; the concertina time of our lives. As such, time contracts and dilates, is arrested and quickened, stretched and compressed, according to the determining vagaries of our experience. It can seem more or less vital, it can be replayed and repeated, it might be meaning-replete or meaning-bereft, for we each of us have experienced useful and useless use of time. When I touch upon 'the concertina time of our lives' above, rather inadvertently but fortuitously, the image of the concertina brings to mind Catherine Clément's study of 'syncope'.[2]

For Clément, syncopal objects include fans and accordions; objects in which operational parts appear and disappear, and this is precisely the source of their fascination. This germinal book takes as its focus the fitful disappearance of the subject. This disappearance isn't always, or necessarily, a bad thing. Indeed, a state of rapture might occasionally ensue as a reward which lies in wait for the unsuspecting subject; the one whose very subjecthood has been (temporarily) placed under threat. Syncope speaks of absence, of a loss of consciousness: *tomber en syncope* means to faint in French, it also refers to musical syncopation. It is an instant when time falters. It is a lacuna in duration. Syncope militates against the seductions of an apparently inexorable flow of time. It serves to remind us that the day will come when this flow will be arrested for good. It is a temporal *memento mori*. Syncope represents a cut in time, but it can also animate time as in musical syncopation or poetry; syncope gives birth to rhythm. In our day-to-day lives, we experience occasions when fragments of time disappear, drop from sight; according to Clément, certain bodily convulsions such as coughing, sneezing and laughter fall within the continuum of syncope. She also instructs us that syncope is derived from *sun* (with) and *kopto* (I cut); more importantly, it is presented as a moment of weakness or passivity from which a new strength emerges and surges forth. It is an eclipse, a moment of *désetre* or unbeing; a moment when the subject temporarily disappears. The 'cut' in time makes its appearance, or, perhaps, more appropriately, its disappearance, in one of its most culturally significant forms in film and video, contemporary collage mediums, where the cut emerges as the most fundamental of structuring devices. In particular, it is the special advantage of video which makes it possible for us, or even, it could be said, obliges us, to enact the compulsion to repeat, thus ... reliving time that has disappeared...[3]

It is this very possibility of reliving disappeared time which makes us acutely aware of time's discontinuity, its faltering, its lacunae, and signals to us that when we 'lose time' there is a concomitant loss of the subject. I am reminded here of *Fistula*, a work where, intermittently, the screen falls blank, black, and acts as an organising and rhythmical syncope.

RELIVING TIME THAT HAS DISAPPEARED...

This fragment of a phrase proposes itself, quite unexpectedly, as the recurrent refrain of this text; it touches upon our compulsion to relive; to repossess; to recover; to resurrect and restore; to raise again and again this disappeared time. In so doing, we strive to raise time from the dead, to recover our pasts. Given this fixation with reliving time, ironically, our greatest folly perhaps, is to inculcate a murderous relation to time. *Ammazare il tempo*. It is after all, our greatest foe and we talk of 'killing time' when in fact, it surreptitiously kills us while we are killing it. And of course, time kills time itself. Killing time might be better thought of as outlining, defining, or marking out parenthetically as it were, an area of 'dead life' or a kind of radical (and sometimes threatening) ennui where meaning is silently drained from existence. It is these scattered areas of 'dead life', where Eros and Thanatos fitfully combine, which offer the clue to one of the key paradoxes of time and reminds us with a just measure of cruelty that:

> Being alternately loses and wins time; consciousness is realised or is dissolved in it. It is therefore quite impossible to experience time totally in the present...[4]

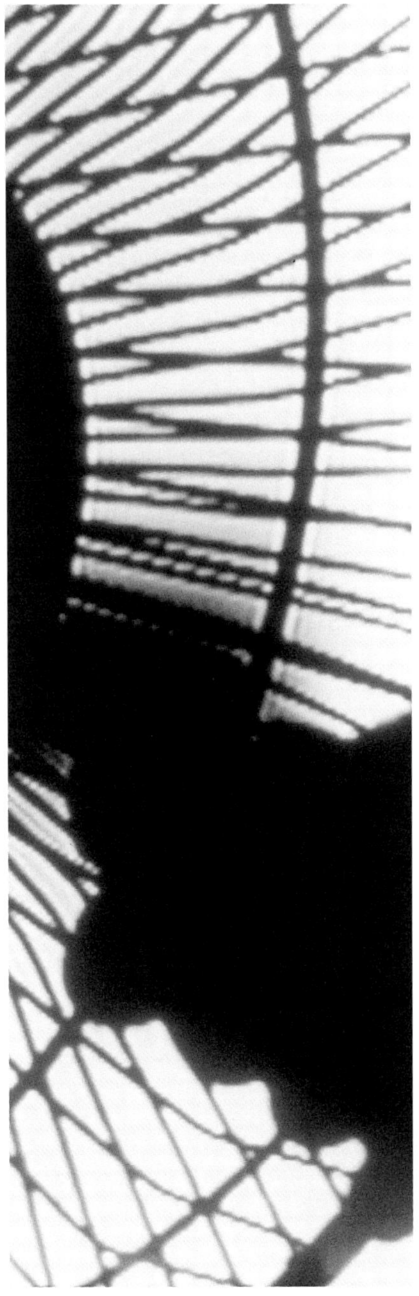

Time then, as we experience it, always carries over a scrap of past dead time into the present and the present contains within it the heartbeat of the immediate future. Consequently, we have an oscillating and ambivalent relation to time, we either defend ourselves from it or take full advantage of it, whichever way we respond is largely dependent on whether we are in what Gaston Bachelard calls 'empty duration or the realising instant'.[5]

Time might equally be experienced as the most deadening of weights/waits or as the most inconspicuous companion blessed by levity and grace. What is sure, however, is that what I can know of time is the pulsional time of embodied time, time made incarnate. It is this currency of embodied time in which the video works of Michael Curran trade and is the poignant remainder I am most able to recall when the image in all its splendour and particularity has long since faded from my screen.

A conspicuous and recurrent theme, device or preoccupation in much of Curran's work is that of repetition. When repetition enters the frame, it is hard to avoid making reference to Gilles Deleuze's work on Sacher-Masoch.[6] This work provides a compelling take on Freud's elaboration of the compulsion to repeat in 'Beyond the Pleasure Principle'. In this work, Freud considers repetition alongside (and necessarily attached to) his foundational formulations of the drives of Eros and Thanatos. For Deleuze, repetition itself was to assume the status of a fundamental force, and became identified as a 'synthesis of time, a "transcendental" synthesis of time.'[7]

This understanding of repetition as a synthesis of time serves to remind us that neither Eros nor Thanatos can be experienced separately or purely, but invariably present themselves to us in differing concentrates and combinations.

> Eros is an ever-repeating synthesis which constitutes the present, but Eros only emerges against the background of the larger field of the pure form of time. That field is the groundless dimension of Thanatos, a dimension convulsed by an incessant repetition of a simultaneous past, present and future.[8]

Embodied or incarnated time in Michael Curran's work is most palpably brought to the fore in the works which themselves feature the artist's body as both instrument and protagonist. These works (for example, *All my little ducks*, *Amami se vuoi*, *L'heure autosexuelle* and *Portfolio*) begin to configure a kind of Foucauldian ethics where the self is realised and shaped, made and remade, as the body itself is disciplined and fashioned through a series of self-realising/self-threatening, strenuously repeated ascetic exercises which, in unanticipated ways, serve to expand our libidinal capabilities. (I would like to cite in passing an early work by Curran, *Panopticon*, 1991, which is clearly indebted to Foucault's writing). Paradoxically, it is this flexing and re-flexing of the musculature of the subject, this strenuous assertion of the self, this testing of the subject to its limits, again and again, which may well result in syncope. I am thinking here, for example, of some of the more extreme ascetic forms of askesis practised in India which have their sacred origins in philosophical traditions of renunciation. I also have in mind the video piece, *All my little ducks*, where Curran, kneeling on a riverbank, repeatedly submerges his head in a basin of water, as if ducking for apples. Each time he holds his breath to the point of near asphyxiation or drowning, only to emerge at the last moment, gasping for breath, drawing back from the very brink of syncope. In common with much of his work, it involves an act of considerable physical exertion, which can be particularly painful or disturbing to witness. The pain or discomfort produced might equally derive from empathy or repulsion, or a bewildering mix of the two. The disturbance induced often serves to heighten the viewer's awareness of time and even relatively short durations can be difficult to bear as time is stretched beyond endurance. These physical exertions stand as inventive modes of modern askesis. This is not too fanciful a suggestion, as Foucault himself was to famously propose, among other disciplines, body building, philosophy and homosexuality as contemporary modes of askesis. These practices were to assume a powerful ethical force in the still unfolding and abruptly interrupted project of Foucault's late work.

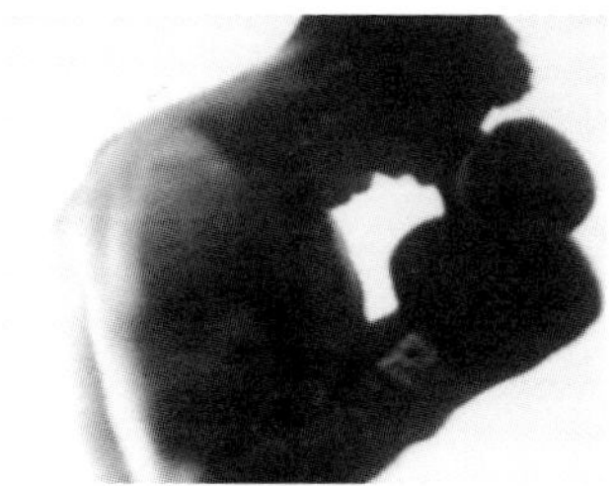

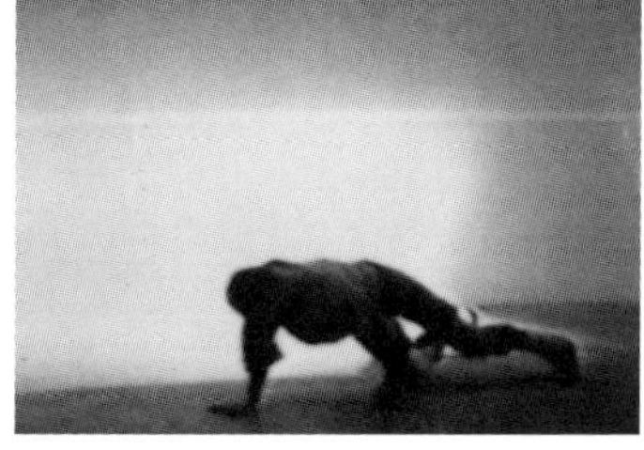

I am pressed here to ask the following question, a question which may not be readily answered, but which is nevertheless worth posing. Can we begin to think here of the emergence of an ethics of time in Curran's work? In order to begin to consider time in this way, we would need to recognise and accept that Eros and Thanatos are powerful determinants which bind time to the subject and the subject to time. Certainly, if we are susceptible to thinking about time (and repetition in particular) in terms which implicate Eros and Thanatos, then I would propose that we might also accept that time itself is necessarily

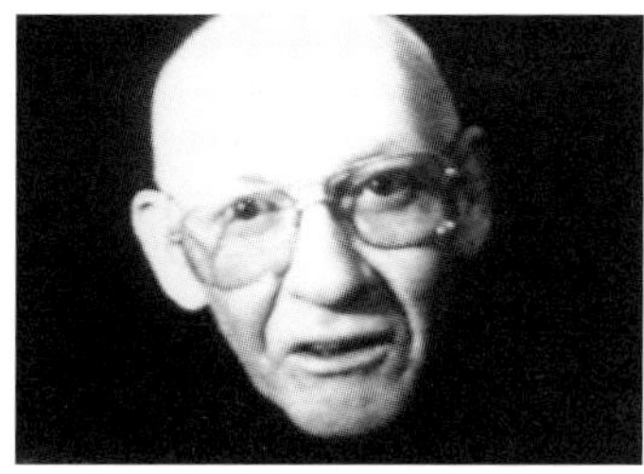

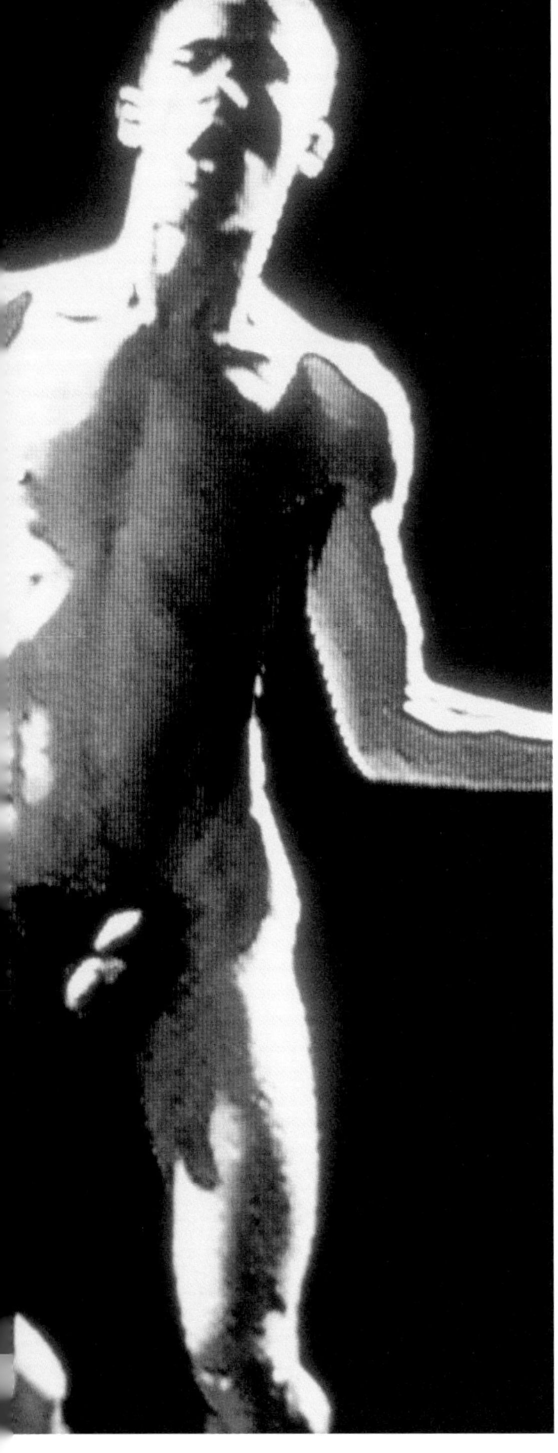

libidinised. We thus come to appreciate time's pulsional dimension; those periods when time is propelled by the drives. The saturated sense of embodied time which surfaces from these practices of reiterated askesis, where repetition itself is made manifest as a fundamental force, would suggest that these forms of repeated temporalities in themselves become libidinised, eroticised, even fetishised, through the very act of repetition. Thanks largely to its determinant technical characteristics, video is peculiarly predisposed to invite, encourage or induce repetition. It also raises the troubling spectre of the possibility of endlessly reliving blocks of time which have disappeared. The video work can be played and replayed, fast forwarded, freeze framed and endlessly rewound, always representing the same sequence, the same transmitted reflection. Or rather, the same retrospective reflection, because the video screen or monitor becomes a kind of transmuted mirror, a kind of mirror with memory where the rewind button compels us to replay again and again... reliving time that has disappeared.

In particular, I have in mind here the video work where Michael Curran dons drag for *Les souffrances du dubbing* (1994) and repeatedly utters at regular intervals the measured incantation: 'Yes, one can feel nostalgia for a place one has never been.' Mostly however, I would like to suggest that these forms of repetition carry deeply embedded within their compulsive appeal, looming questions to do with the complex processes of sexualisation and desexualisation. Most especially, they invite us to ponder the processes through which the bonds of sexualisation or cathexis are established and subsequently transmute into the loosening effects of desexualisation or decathexis. In order to explore this dynamic of sexualisation and desexualisation a little further, it will serve my purpose to concentrate on one of the most extraordinary and harrowing pieces from Curran's extensive corpus, namely, *Amami se vuoi*, which translates loosely from the Italian as 'Love me if you like'. The work takes its stirring title from a plaintive ballad, a song drenched in longing, which is to be heard as a kind of auditory backdrop to the rather ceremonial or ritualistic encounter which is to be served up to the viewer. We see a naked Curran, in meditative mood. He finishes a cigarette and prepares to take up position, supinate on a table, his legs dangling over the edge. Another male appears and, standing between Curran's legs, he leans over him, pressing genitals to genitals. The scene is set, then shockingly and unexpectedly he begins to spit into Curran's face. He spits into his open eyes and open mouth, we feel the spit hit the back of his throat and ricochet. Curran's gaping mouth reaches for the mouth of the other, apparently seeking tenderness or reconciliation in a kiss. It never reaches its destination. Agape, it is an image we only know from the extremes of our existence; a paroxysm of pleasure; celebratory abandon; a silent cry of despair; or the last throes of death. This distressing scenario articulates, without recourse to language, the paralysing truth of desire. It is the condition of desire that it is condemned to remain thwarted and unfulfilled, trapped in cycle of endless repetition, as desire always fixes its sight upon desire. In *Amami se vuoi*, Curran succeeds in revealing to us a terrible truth about our existence; it is a truth revealed with appropriate coldness and cruelty, but is a truth we need to stare in the face. The pain which suffuses and structures this piece is the pain of identity, the pain of desire; it shows us a pain deeply inscribed in subjectivity. It is a sado-masochistic scenario which displays the truth of a queering, twisting, perversion of desire whereby, with the force of monumental revelation, we find:

> Eros is desexualized and humiliated for the sake of a resexualized Thanatos.[9]

Much has been written on the still photograph's complex relation to themes of time and memory and, most especially, its intimate relation with death; so much so, that the term thanatography might well be proposed to better articulate the narration of this morbid proximity. The fall of the camera shutter is, in itself, a form of syncope. Recognising this dubiously privileged status of photography, Laura Mulvey highlights two differing theoretical responses to this relation to death when she tells us:

> For both Barthes and Bazin, photography's inscription in time, its actual literalness, touches on essential human aspiration to do with death. For Bazin, it is to transcend death; for Barthes, it is the dive into death.[10]

The moving video image would, on the face of it, lend itself less readily to such theoretical associations, due in part, I suppose, to dynamic qualities such as movement and speed, forms of quickness most usually taken to be life-affirming attributes; signifiers of vivification. Yet, I am brought back to my haunting refrain: the iterative notion of ...reliving time that has disappeared... and it is precisely the possibility of such an event which firmly establishes the thanatographic dimension of this time-based/time-bound practice. It seems only just that, by way of bringing this text to a close, I offer the full phrase of this tantalising refrain, which simply unfurls a poignant reminder:

> Thus, reliving time that has disappeared means learning the disquiet of our own death.[11]

The task remains for each of us to determine whether this reminder prompts a plunge into the lugubrious depths of death or, by contrast, acts as a spur to transcendence.

1 Gaston Bachelard, *The Dialectic of Duration*, Clinamen Press, Manchester, 2000, p 51.

2 Catherine Clément, *Syncope: The Philosophy of Rapture*, University of Minnesota Press, Minneapolis and London, 1994.

3 Gaston Bachelard, *The Dialectic of Duration*, Clinamen Press, Manchester, 2000, p 51

4 Ibid, p 50.

5 Ibid, p 50.

6 Gilles Deleuze, *Masochism*, Zone Books, New York, 1991.

7 Cited by Ronald Bogue, *Deleuze and Guattari*, Routledge, London and New York, 1989, p 52.

8 Ibid, p 53.

9 Cited by Ronald Bogue, *Deleuze and Guattari*, Routledge, London and New York, 1989, p 53.

10 Laura Mulvey, 'The Index and the Uncanny', *Time and the Image*, (Ed.), Carolyn Bailey Gill, Manchester University Press, Manchester and New York, 2000, p 144.

11 Gaston Bachelard, *The Dialectic of Duration*, Clinamen Press, Manchester, 2000, p 51.

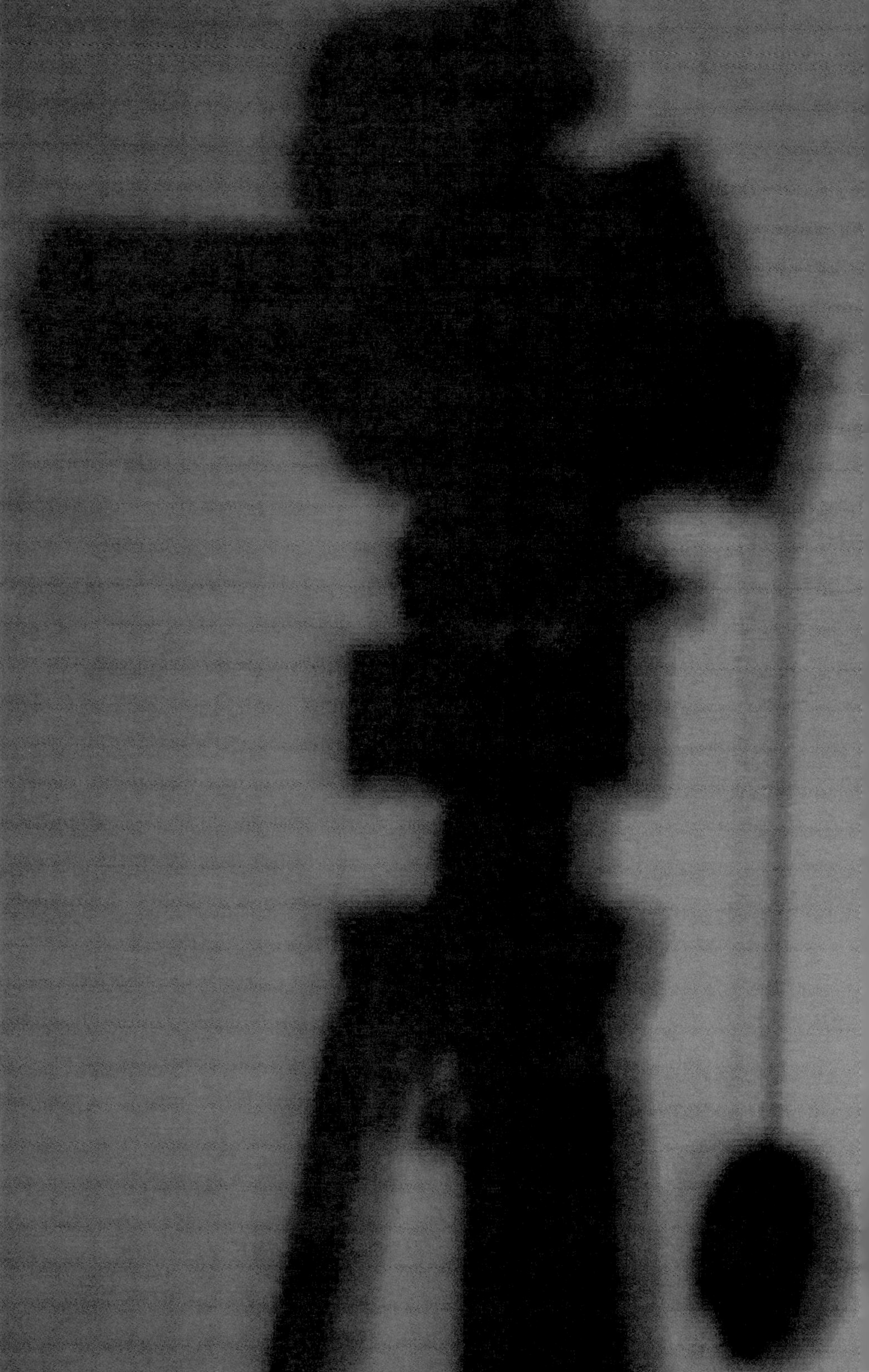

lists

Michael Curran

1963	Born, Scotland
1988 - 1991	Goldsmiths College, London, B.A. Fine Art
1992 - 1993	Duncan of Jordanstone College of Art, Dundee, Electronic Imaging PG Dip
1993 - 1995	Jan Van Eyck Akademie, Centre for Post-graduate Study, Maastricht

EXHIBITIONS AND SCREENINGS

2003 *Love In A Cold Climate*, Rotterdam Film Festival

2002 'Better Than the Real Thing', Smart project space, Amsterdam

2001 'Dead Wall Reverie', Five Years Gallery, London
'The Scottish Play', Hoxton Distilleries, London
'Radio Skylark', Fordhams Space, London

2000 'Nightclub Robberies', Rhodes + Mann Gallery, London
'The Red Room', Five Years Gallery, London
'Video Positive 2000: The Other Side of Zero', Bluecoat Gallery, Liverpool
'Closing/Close By', Spacex Gallery, Exeter

1999 'Videostore', Espace Des Arts, Chalon-sur-Saone, France
'New Video from Great Britain', British Council Touring Programme to various venues in South America
'Mix Brazil Festival', Sao Paolo
'Image Forum', Tokyo, Osaka, Fukuoka, London
'Magnetic North', Film and Video Umbrella Touring Programme, Newcastle, Trondheim, Hexham, London
'Unconditional Love', Oslo

1998 'New Video from Great Britain', Museum of Modern Art, New York
'IF 6 WAS 9', Cinema Rex, Belgrade
'The Kindness of Strangers', W139 Gallery, Amsterdam
'Bruno Gironcolli & Michael Curran', Galerie Jamarr, Antwerp
'Toronto Film Festival', Toronto

1997 'Corps Perdu', STUK, Leuven
'Festival du Nouveaux Cinema', Quebec
'Prend Garde!', J. Grimonprez Video Library, Documenta X, Kassel
'Pictures of Lily', Underwood St Gallery, London

1996 'Male Performance', W139 Gallery, Amsterdam
'Speed', Tullie House Museum, Carlisle
'Pandaemonium', Institute of Contemporary Arts, London
'I Beg to Differ', Milch Gallery, London
'Make Me Clean Again', Alpenmilchzentrale, Vienna
'Foreign Body', Museum for Gegenwartskunst, Basel
'Monstrosities', Kleines Festival der Hackeschen Höfe, Berlin
'Perfect', Galerie Mot & van den Boogard, Brussels
'Movimento', Reina Sofia, Madrid

1995 'Exotic Excursions', Fouberts Place, London
'What You See Is What You Get', 3rd ICA Biennale, London, Tokyo, Sydney, New York
'Auto Reverse - Video and Psychoanalysis', Saint Gervais, Geneva, Switzerland
'How is Everything?' Wiener Secession, Vienna, Landesmuseum, Innsbruck,
'Masculin/Feminin X/Y', Centre Georges Pompidou, Paris
'Instant', Camden Arts Centre, London

1994 'This Side of The Channel', Institute of Contemporary Arts, London
'European Media Art Festival', Osnabrück
'The British Short Film Festival', London
'11th Kasseler Dokumentarfilm & Videofestival', Filmladen Kassel
'Points de Vue: Image d'Europe', Centre Georges Pompidou, Paris

IN COLLECTION

Centre Georges Pompidou, Nouveaux Media: *L'heure autosexuelle*, *Amami se Vuoi*, *Disclaimer*
Artothek Vienna: *Das Pelzchen*

SELECTED PUBLICATIONS

The Pursuit of the Personal in British Video Art, Catherine Elwes
Directory of British Film & Video Artists, editor David Curtis
Pictures of Lily, editor Jeremy Akerman
Closing / Close By, Chris Darke, Imogen Stidworthy and Michael Curran

AWARDS

1995 2nd Prix de Geneve for *Fistula*, in collaboration with Osnat Haber
1991 BP EXPO Award for *The Small Boy's Dream*